Iron *Sharpens* Iron

Letters From the pen of Gerri Nash

Iron *Sharpens* Iron

Letters From the pen of Gerri Nash

by

Gerri Nash

Christian Outreach Ministries Evangelist
P. O. Box 581942
Tulsa, Oklahoma 74158-1942

Unless otherwise indicated, all Scripture quotations are taken from the *King James Version* of the Bible.

1st *Printing*

Iron Sharpens Iron: Letters From the pen of Gerri Nash
ISBN 0-9649747-3-8
Copyright © 2004 by Gerri Nash
P.O. Box 581942
Tulsa, Oklahoma 74158-1942

Published by **Christian Outreach Ministries Evangelist**
P.O. Box 581942
Tulsa, Oklahoma 74158-1942
918.496.9555

www.comeministries.org

Printed in the United States of America. All rights reserved under International Copyright Law. Contents and/or cover may not be reproduced in whole or in part in any form without the express written consent of the Publisher.

Contents

Dedication

Acknowledgements

Forward

Introduction

1. Good Success.. 1
2. The Prince Of Peace.. 2
3. God Sent His Word To Heal Us.. 3
4. Never Give Up On Your Dreams...................................... 4
5. Living The Good Life.. 5
6. A Merry Heart.. 6
7. God Is For You.. 7
8. The Power Of The Tongue... 8
9. The Greatest Expression Of Love.................................... 9
10. God Wants Us To Succeed... 10
11. A Life Of Abundance... 11
12. A Path Of Light.. 12
13. Working Our Faith... 13
14. The God Kind Of Love.. 14
15. What Are You Thinking?... 15
16. Divine Love.. 16
17. The Fruit Of Our Labor... 17
18. Be A Person Of Your Word.. 18
19. Is Christ In Your Christmas?.. 19
20. Blessed!... 20
21. We Don't Have To Fear.. 21
22. We Serve The Mighty God... 22
23. Benefits.. 23

Contents

24. Worship God..	24
25. God Is Our Source..	25
26. A Good Work..	26
27. Living A Long Life...	27
28. Doing Impossible Things...	28
29. The Favor Of God...	29
30. Just Do Good..	30
31. God Is More Than Enough...	31
32. The Holiday Season..	32
33. God Is Faithful...	33
34. The Integrity Of God's Word..	34
35. Let Your Light Shine...	35
36. The Heart Of God...	36
37. It's Possible!	37
38. A New Millennium..	38
39. Don't Try To Get Rich Too Fast...................................	39
40. The Best Is Yet To Come!	40
41. God's Word Will Bring You Life...................................	41
42. The Outward Workings Of Love.................................	42
43. Working The Word Of God...	43
44. Jesus Is The Healer..	44
45. Walking In Favor...	45

Conclusion

About The Author

Product Information

I dedicate this book to my mother, Louise Harris,
and in memory of my father, William Harris.

Also to my husband, Corbin, and my daughter, Adia,
my sisters, Goldan Jean, Linda, and Gloria Marie, and my brothers,
Raymond, Ronnie Paul, and Russell.

Acknowledgments

First, I want to give honor to God my Father for His Word, which is a lamp to my feet and light to my path.

I want to thank my husband, Corbin, and daughter, Adia, for encouraging me to take a step of faith to publish my writings to bless the Body of Christ.

I also want to thank my friend, Dr. Allean Varnado, for encouraging and inspiring me.

I am grateful to my sister, Gloria Marie, who has taken upon herself to distribute our monthly letters to her co-workers, strangers, and friends.

I am also grateful to my niece, Johnette Winfrey, for her encouragement along the way and her thoughtful emails.

I am extremely grateful to my mother, Louise Harris, whom I love and appreciate so much. She raised us in the church and taught us to honor God. Much of the material in these letters has come out of the many conversations we had over the years.

Foreward

With the many demands of today's society, people are not in the habit of setting time aside to read and meditate on the things of God. Several years ago, I had an opportunity to give a Christian book to a former co-worker. This book contained about fifty pages. After a month, I noticed that this person still had the book on his desk. I also noticed that many pages were marked and highlighted, which showed me that he had an interest in the book.

I concluded, that he just couldn't or wouldn't allocate the time to read the book in one setting. I assumed that he only took time to read a few pages a day, because he was too busy. His life and job demanded most of his time. Many people today are so busy, that they will not commit to anything that will interrupt their schedule.

In an attempt to compete with the many challenges of our monthly mail recipients, my wife began to write a one-page letter each month. We were surprised at the overwhelming response we received. That was over four years ago, and we are still sending out the "Letter of The Month". These letters are short and powerful and they are *full* of God's Word.

Over the years, many have testified about the power in this one-page letter. These letters are also used in many churches and Bible study groups all over the country. It is my hope that this book will continue to bless even more people. In this book, Iron *Sharpens* Iron, my wife has compiled 45 of her most treasured letters. She has done a wonderful job of compiling this information in a way that will bless you and your family. Read them and be blessed!

Rev. Corbin N. Nash, Pastor
COME Church
Tulsa, Oklahoma

Introduction

For many years, I used to write my mother on a monthly basis to encourage her in the things of God. Every month, I would write about a different subject [healing, long life, fear, prosperity, and so on], along with scriptural references. I would include many scriptures in my letter to enhance her daily devotion. She looked forward to receiving those letters, because they kept her encouraged and inspired.

One day my husband and I were discussing some things that we can do to bless the people on our mailing list. We decided that sending out a monthly letter would encourage and inspire them. Over four years ago, we sent out the first "Letter of the Month". We received so many overwhelming and positive responses; we decided to continue the mailings, even to this day.

Iron *Sharpens* Iron is a book that contains many of the letters that we've distributed. They contain words of encouragement, motivation, inspiration and healing, as well as being full of the Word of God. Proverbs 27:17 says, "Iron sharpeneth iron; so a man sharpeneth the countenance of his friend."

I pray that this book will help you, sharpen you, and transform your life.

— Gerri Nash

Iron *Sharpens* Iron

Study Notes

Additional Scripture References:
_____
_____
_____
_____
_____

Notes:
_____
_____
_____
_____
_____
_____
_____
_____
_____
_____
_____
_____
_____
_____
_____
_____

Iron *Sharpens* Iron

Good Success

Dear Friend:

I remember when I used to write to my mother to encourage her in the things of God. She always looked forward to receiving my letters, because they would encourage her to get into the Word of God [the Bible]. My mother would read and meditate upon the Scriptures that were included in the letter. She would actually read the letter, read the Scriptures and meditate upon them everyday until she received my next letter.

God told Joshua to meditate upon the Word of God and it will cause him to prosper and have good success (Joshua 1:8). What did God mean when He told Joshua to meditate? "Meditate" means *to study and reflect upon, to mutter, to utter*. Joshua had faith, and he did what God told him to do. As a result of Joshua's obedience, he was able to enter into the Promised Land and posses it.

If we want to prosper and have good success, we must study and reflect upon the Word, we must mutter the Word and utter the Word. As we obey God and do what He tells us to do in His Word, we will enjoy life and have good success.

Joshua 1:8 says, "This book of the law shall not depart out of thy mouth; but thou shalt meditate therein day and night, that thou mayest observe to do according to all that is written therein: for then thou shalt make thy way prosperous, and then thou shalt have good success."

Psalm 1:1-3 says, "Blessed is the man that walketh not in the counsel of the ungodly, nor standeth in the way of sinners, nor sitteth in the seat of the scornful. But his delight is in the law of the Lord; and in his law doth he meditate day and night. And he shall be like a tree planted by the rivers of water, that bringeth forth his fruit in his season; his leaf also shall not wither; and whatsoever he doeth shall prosper."

Deuteronomy 28:12,13 says, "The Lord shall open unto thee his good treasure, the heaven to give the rain unto thy land in his season, and to bless all the work of thine hand: and thou shalt lend unto many nations, and thou shalt not borrow. And the Lord shall make thee the head, and not the tail; and thou shalt be above only, and thou shalt not be beneath; if that thou hearken unto the commandments of the Lord thy God, which I command thee this day, to observe and to do them."

Proverbs 15:6 says, "In the house of the righteous is much treasure: but in the revenues of the wicked is trouble."

Job 22:28 says, "Thou shalt also decree a thing, and it shall be established unto thee: and the light shall shine upon thy ways."

Remember, God wants us to enter into and possess our *Promised Land*.

Iron *Sharpens* Iron

Study Notes

Additional Scripture References:

Notes:

Iron *Sharpens* Iron

The Prince Of Peace

Dear Friend:

We are living in a time where there is turmoil and trouble all around us. So many people are afraid, worried, frustrated, and confused. They are in strife and contention with their friends and loved ones. When they go to bed at night, they can't sleep, because their spirits are vexed. They don't have any peace.

God wants us to live in peace. This is why He sent His Son [Jesus] to the earth. Jesus came to the earth to bring us peace. He is called the *"Prince of Peace"* (Isaiah 9:6). When we have peace, we have *quietness, tranquility, wholeness,* and *completeness.*

If we know Jesus as our Lord and Savior, we have the Prince of Peace living on the inside of us. If we are not experiencing peace, it's because we have not allowed the Prince of Peace to work in our lives. We can do this by simply praying and believing this prayer:

> *Lord Jesus, I acknowledge You as the Prince of Peace.*
> *I'm asking You to be the Prince of Peace in my life.*
> *Thank You Lord for working in my life as my Prince of Peace.*

Isaiah 9:6 says, "For unto us a child is born, unto us a son is given: and the government shall be upon his shoulder: and his name shall be called Wonderful, Counsellor, The mighty God, The everlasting Father, The Prince of Peace."

John 14:27 says, "Peace I leave with you, my peace I give unto you: not as the world giveth, give I unto you. Let not your heart be troubled, neither let it be afraid."

Psalm 4:8 says, "I will both lay me down in peace, and sleep: for thou, Lord, only makest me dwell in safety."

2 Thessalonians 3:16 says, "Now the Lord of peace himself give you peace always by all means. The Lord be with you all."

Philippians 4:6,7 says, "Be careful for nothing; but in every thing by prayer and supplication with thanksgiving let your requests be made known unto God. And the peace of God, which passeth all understanding, shall keep your hearts and minds through Christ Jesus."

Proverbs 3:1,2 says, "My son, forget not my law; but let thine heart keep my commandments: For length of days, and long life, and peace, shall they add to thee."

Colossians 3:15 says, "And let the peace of God rule in your hearts, to the which also ye are called in one body; and be ye thankful."

Remember, Jesus is our *"Prince of Peace"*.

Iron *Sharpens* Iron

Study Notes

Additional Scripture References:

Notes:

Iron *Sharpens* Iron

God Sent His Word To Heal Us

Dear Friend:

Today many people are sick and afraid that they may die at an early age. Some may even think that there is a curse of sickness upon them and their loved ones. As Christians, we need not be afraid of sickness, because Jesus has redeemed us from the curse of sickness. Jesus wants us healed, and He wants us whole. Jesus wants us to live a long and full life.

The Bible tells us that God sent His word to heal us and to deliver us from our destructions (Psalm 107:20). Today I am sending you God's Word so that you can be healed and delivered from all of your destructions.

Galatians 3:13 says, "Christ hath redeemed us from the curse of the law, being made a curse for us: for it is written, Cursed is every one that hangeth on a tree."

Mark 5:36 says, ". . . Be not afraid, only believe."

Proverbs 4:20-22 says, "My son [or daughter], attend to my words; incline thine ear unto my sayings. Let them not depart from thine eyes; keep them in the midst of thine heart. For they are life unto those that find them, and health to all their flesh."

Deuteronomy 7:15 says, "And the Lord will take away from thee all sickness, and will put none [permit none] of the evil diseases of Egypt, which thou knowest, upon thee."

Deuteronomy 11:21 says, "That your days may be multiplied, and the days of your children, in the land which the Lord sware unto your fathers to give them, as the days of heaven upon earth."

Ephesians 6:1-3 says, "Children, obey your parents in the Lord: for this is right. Honour thy father and mother; which is the first commandment with promise; That it may be well with thee, and thou mayest live long on the earth."

Proverbs 9:11 says, "For by me thy days shall be multiplied, and the years of thy life shall increased."

Jeremiah 30:17 says, "For I will restore health unto thee, and I will heal thee of thy wounds, saith the Lord."

Joel 3:10 says, ". . .Let the weak say, I am strong."

Matthew 8:17 says, "That it might be fulfilled which was spoken by Esaias the prophet saying, Himself took our infirmities, and bare our sicknesses."

1 Peter 2:24 says, "Who his own self bare our sins in his own body on the tree, that we, being dead to sins, should live unto righteousness: by whose stripes ye were healed."

Remember, God sent *His Word* to heal and deliver us.

Iron *Sharpens* Iron

Study Notes

Additional Scripture References:

Notes:

Iron *Sharpens* Iron

Never Give Up On Your Dreams

Dear Friend:

I want to encourage you to never give up on your dreams. Some of you probably are saying, "Okay, but I've been waiting for a long time for my dreams to come into reality". If we have faith and confidence in God and His Word [the Bible], He'll surely bring our dreams into reality. Habakkuk 2:2,3 in *The Amplified Bible* says, ". . . Write the vision and engrave it so plainly upon tablets that everyone who passes may [be able to] read [it easily and quickly] as he hastens by. For the vision is yet for an appointed time and it hastens to the end [fulfillment]; it will not deceive or disappoint. Though it tarry, wait [earnestly] for it, because it will surely come; it will not be behindhand on its appointed day."

The devil will bring distractions, discouragement, and depression to try and make us give up on our dreams, but we shouldn't give the devil any place. We shouldn't let anyone or any circumstance that we encounter, make us turn loose of our dreams. We must believe that we can achieve and be successful in every area of our lives. So we should stop listening to negative talk, and stop looking at the circumstances around us. We must believe and trust the Lord to bring our dreams into reality, and one day our dreams will be a reality. God delights in bringing our dreams into reality.

Habakkuk 2:2,3 says, "And the Lord answered me, and said, Write the vision, and make it plain upon tables, that he may run that readeth it. For the vision is yet for an appointed time, but at the end it shall speak, and not lie: though it tarry, wait for it; because it will surely come, it will not tarry."

Psalm 126:1-3 says, "When the Lord turned again the captivity of Zion, we were like them that dream. Then was our mouth filled with laughter, and our tongue with singing: then said they among the heathen, The Lord hath done great things for them. The Lord hath done great things for us; whereof we are glad."

Galatians 6:9 says, "And let us not be weary in well doing: for in due season we shall reap, if we faint not."

Psalm 37:4,5 says, "Delight thyself also in the Lord; and he shall give thee the desires of thine heart. Commit thy way unto the Lord; trust also in him; and he shall bring it to pass."

Psalm 138:8 says, "The Lord will perfect that which concerneth me: thy mercy, O Lord, endureth for ever: forsake not the works of thine own hands."

Mark 9:23 says, "Jesus said unto him, If thou canst believe, all things are possible to him that believeth."

Remember to never give up on your dreams.

Iron *Sharpens* Iron

Study Notes

Additional Scripture References:

Notes:

Iron *Sharpens* Iron

Living The Good Life

Dear Friend:

God has provided all of the instructions we need to have a prosperous life. These instructions are clearly written in the Word of God [the Bible]. So many of us are living below our means as children of God. Some of us are at the bottom of the barrel, scrapping whatever we can find. There are others of us, who are living from paycheck to paycheck. We are in so much debt, we can't see any way out.

Our Heavenly Father doesn't want us to live that way. He wants us to live the good life, having all of our needs met. If we do what the Word of God tells us to do, we'll find ourselves rising above poverty into the life that God wants us to live.

As we meditate upon the Scriptures below, they will become alive in us, and we'll begin to see our financial situations changing, living the life that God wants us to live.

Psalm 37:18,19 says, "The Lord knoweth the days of the upright: and their inheritance shall be forever. They shall not be ashamed in the evil time: and in the days of famine they shall be satisfied."

Philippians 4:19 says, "But my God shall supply all your need according to his riches in glory by Christ Jesus."

Psalm 34:10 says, "The young lions do lack, and suffer hunger: but they that seek the Lord shall not want any good thing."

Luke 6:38 says, "Give, and it shall be given unto you; good measure, pressed down, and shaken together, and running over, shall men give into your bosom. For with the same measure that ye mete withal it shall be measured to you again."

Psalm 23:1 says, "The Lord is my shepherd; I shall not want."

2 Corinthians 9:6 says, "But this I say, He which soweth sparingly shall reap also sparingly; and he which soweth bountifully shall reap also bountifully."

Proverbs 11:24,25 says, "There is that scattereth, and yet increaseth; and there is that withholdeth more than is meet, but it tendeth to poverty. The liberal soul shall be made fat: and he that watereth shall be watered also himself."

Job 36:11 says, "If they obey and serve him, they shall spend their days in prosperity, and their years in pleasures."

Deuteronomy 28:2-6 says, "And all these blessings shall come on thee, and overtake thee, if thou shalt hearken unto the voice of the Lord thy God. Blessed shalt thou be in the city, and blessed shalt thou be in the field. Blessed shall be the fruit of thy body, and the fruit of thy ground, and the fruit of thy cattle, the increase of thy kine, and the flocks of thy sheep. Blessed shall be thy basket and thy store. Blessed shalt thou be when thou comest in, and blessed shalt thou be when thou goest out."

Remember, God wants us to live the "*good life*".

Iron *Sharpens* Iron

Study Notes

Additional Scripture References:

Notes:

Iron *Sharpens* Iron

A Merry Heart

Dear Friend:

A merry heart is just like medicine. Medical Science has discovered that people who are happy and laugh most of the time, heal faster than those who are depressed and sad. Medical Science has even discovered that people who laugh, and are positive, live longer than those who are sad and depressed most of the time. What Medical Science found was in the Bible all of the time. Proverbs 17:22 says, "A merry heart doeth good like a medicine: but a broken spirit drieth the bones."

Joy and laughter can do more for us than any drug. Having a merry and a joyful heart is a great remedy for stress and anxiety. Joy and laughter increase circulation, lower blood pressure, and reduce muscle tension and wrinkles in the face. Have you ever wondered why God said so many times in His Word [the Bible] to rejoice? God knows that being merry and joyful, works wonders for our soul and body. God wants us to be happy.

Do you know that we can laugh our way to victory, and we can laugh our way to health? So put off that pickled face and sad countenance, and take a dose of joy and laughter. Everyday we should take a dose of joy and laughter. It'll work wonders for our soul and body.

Proverbs 15:13,15 says, "A merry heart maketh a cheerful countenance: but by sorrow of the heart the spirit is broken. All the days of the afflicted are evil: but he that is of a merry heart hath a continual feast."

Psalm 35:9 says, "And my soul shall be joyful in the Lord: it shall rejoice in his salvation."

James 5:13 says, "Is any among you afflicted? let him pray. Is any merry? let him sing psalms."

Psalm 32:11 says, "Be glad in the Lord, and rejoice, ye righteous: and shout for joy, all ye that are upright in heart."

Psalm 98:4 says, "Make a joyful noise unto the Lord, all the earth: make a loud noise, and rejoice, and sing praise."

Philippians 4:4 says, "Rejoice in the Lord alway: and again I say, Rejoice."

Psalm 5:11,12 says, "But let all those that put their trust in thee rejoice: let them ever shout for joy, because thou defendest them: let them also that love thy name be joyful in thee. For thou, Lord, wilt bless the righteous; with favour wilt thou compass him as with a shield."

Remember, we can't overdose on joy and laughter.

Iron *Sharpens* Iron

Study Notes

Additional Scripture References:

Notes:

Iron *Sharpens* Iron

God Is For You

Dear Friend:

Do you know that God is for you? God is for you, and He's more than the whole world against you. God is for you, and He's greater than the whole world against you. I've once heard a minister say, "If God is for you, it doesn't matter who's against you". What a deep and sobering saying!

It doesn't matter who betrays you. It doesn't matter who says bad things about you. It doesn't matter who tries to ruin your reputation. It doesn't matter who sets background plots against you. It doesn't matter who tries to hold you back. It doesn't matter who tries to keep you from succeeding in life. If God is for you, no one can succeed being against you.

Sometimes it may seem that God is far from us, and He doesn't hear us when we cry out to Him for help. My friend, I assure you that God does hear us when we cry out to Him. He doesn't only hear us, but He's willingly ready to help us and deliver us. No matter what we are going through, He'll lift us up and bring us out into victory. We must believe and trust Him to do it.

Romans 8:31 says, "What shall we then say to these things? If God be for us, who can be against us?"

1 John 4:4 says, "Ye are of God, little children, and have overcome them: because greater is he that is in you, than he that is in the world."

Isaiah 40:29,31 says, "He giveth power to the faint; and to them that have no might he increaseth strength. But they that wait upon the Lord shall renew their strength; they shall mount up with wings as eagles; they shall run, and not be weary; and they shall walk, and not faint."

Habakkuk 3:19 says, "The Lord God is my strength, and he will make my feet like hinds' feet, and he will make me to walk upon mine high places. To the chief singer on my stringed instruments."

Isaiah 41:10-13 says, "Fear thou not; for I am with thee: be not dismayed; for I am thy God: I will strengthen thee; yea, I will help thee; yea, I will uphold thee with the right hand of my righteousness. Behold, all they that were incensed against thee shall be ashamed and confounded: they shall be as nothing; and they that strive with thee shall perish. Thou shalt seek them, and shalt not find them, even them that contended with thee: they that war against thee shall be as nothing, and as a thing of nought. For I the Lord thy God will hold thy right hand, saying unto thee, Fear not; I will help thee."

Remember, God is for you, and He is more than the whole world against you.

Iron *Sharpens* Iron

Study Notes

Additional Scripture References:

Notes:

Iron *Sharpens* Iron

The Power Of The Tongue

Dear Friend:

We can change the course of our lives by our tongue. James 3:2 in *The Amplified Bible* says, "For we all often stumble and fall and offend in many things. And if any one does not offend in speech [never says the wrong things], he is a fully developed character and a perfect man, able to control his whole body and to curb his entire nature." With our tongue, we can speak cursing or blessings into our lives. We should be mindful of the words we speak, because words set the course of our lives.

The tongue is powerful than what most people think. For example, if you speak positive words over your children, they will go out in life's fight and win. But if you speak negative words over your children, they will believe that they can't achieve in life. Children are products of what's spoken in the home. So learn to speak words of life over your children.

Some of us may be wondering why we are not succeeding in life. We should check out our tongue. We should pay attention to what we are saying. We can speak blessings or cursing over our lives. Some of us may have missed it in the past and haven't been speaking blessings over our lives, but we can start today.

James 3:2-6 says, "For in many things we offend all. If any man offend not in word, the same is a perfect man, and able also to bridle the whole body. Behold, we put bits in the horses' mouths, that they may obey us; and we turn about their whole body. Behold also the ships, which though they be so great, and are driven of fierce winds, yet are they turned about with a very small helm, whithersoever the governor listeth. Even so the tongue is a little member, and boasteth great things. Behold, how great a matter a little fire kindleth! And the tongue is a fire, a world of iniquity: so is the tongue among our members, that it defileth the whole body, and setteth on fire the course of nature; and it is set on fire of hell."

Proverbs 18:21 says, "Death and life are in the power of the tongue: and they that love it shall eat the fruit thereof."

Proverbs 12:18 says, "There is that speaketh like the piercings of a sword: but the tongue of the wise is health."

Proverbs 15:4 says, "A wholesome tongue is a tree of life: but perverseness therein is a breach in the spirit."

Matthew 12:37 says, "For by thy words thou shalt be justified, and by thy words thou shalt be condemned."

Romans 4:17 says, ". . . Even God, who quickeneth the dead, and calleth those things which be not as though they were."

Remember, our tongue can produce blessings or cursing.

Iron *Sharpens* Iron

Study Notes

Additional Scripture References:

Notes:

Iron *Sharpens* Iron

The Greatest Expression Of Love

Dear Friend:

Valentines Day is the time of year where everyone celebrates love. Cards, big boxes of candy, flowers, and even expensive pieces of jewelry are given and received by the ones we love, as an expression of our love. But even through our expression of love, we hold animosity, hurt, and offenses.

Have we taken the time out to realize what we are doing? Have we forgiven our loved ones, even though they have wronged and hurt us? Are we still holding grudges? Do we take offense, when our loved ones tell us the truth, and we are too stubborn to change?

God doesn't want us to go around carrying offenses. All of the outward expression of love is worthless and meaningless, if we don't display the God kind of love. The God kind of love doesn't hold hurt and grudges. The God kind of love is willing to change. The God kind of love puts the other person first. The God kind of love takes no offense. The God kind of love isn't selfish. The God kind of love forgives and forgets.

If we haven't been expressing the God kind of love toward our loved ones, we can start by confessing 1 Corinthians 13:4-8 on a daily basis. We shouldn't only show an expression of love once a year, but all throughout the year.

1 Corinthians 13:4-8 (*The Amplified Bible*) says, "Love endures long and is patient and kind; love never is envious nor boils over with jealous, is not boastful or vainglorious, does not display itself haughtily. It is not conceited (arrogant and inflated with pride); it is not rude (unmannerly) and does not act unbecomingly. Love (God's love in us) does not insist on its own rights or its own way, for it is not self-seeking; it is not touchy or fretful or resentful; it takes no account of the evil done to it [it pays no attention to a suffered wrong]. It does not rejoice at injustice and unrighteousness, but rejoices when right and truth prevail. Love bears up under anything and everything that comes, is ever ready to believe the best of every person, its hopes are fadeless under all circumstances, and it endures everything [without weakening]. Love never fails [never fades out or becomes obsolete or comes to an end]."

Galatians 5:13,14 says, "For, brethren, ye have been called unto liberty; only use not liberty for an occasion to the flesh, but by love serve one another. For all the law is fulfilled in one word, even in this; Thou shalt love thy neighbour as thyself."

2 Corinthians 5:14 says, "For the love of Christ constraineth us; because we thus judge, that if one died for all, then were all dead."

Ephesians 5:25 says, "Husbands, love your wives, even as Christ also loved the church, and gave himself for it."

Remember, the God kind of love is the greatest expression of love.

Iron *Sharpens* Iron

Study Notes

Additional Scripture References:
_____
_____
_____
_____
_____

Notes:
_____
_____
_____
_____
_____
_____
_____
_____
_____
_____
_____
_____
_____
_____
_____

Iron *Sharpens* Iron

God Wants Us To Succeed

Dear Friend:

God has plans for us to succeed in life. He has provided everything that we need to be successful, and He has put everything on the inside of us to make us a success. Some of you may be thinking that you are a failure, because you haven't achieved the things in life that you thought that you should've achieved. Others of you may consider yourself a failure, because your dreams and desires haven't yet been manifested. Stop seeing yourself as a failure. Stop telling yourself that you're a failure. God wants us to succeed more than we want to succeed. God hasn't made us a failure. God has made us a success.

As we begin to spend some quiet time with the Lord, reading the Word of God [the Bible], and worshipping Him, He will begin to make Himself known unto us. God will begin to show us success and ways to succeed in life. As we seek the Lord, we will begin to succeed.

Let's make this confession out loud:

> *I am not a failure. I do not have plans to fail.*
> *God has plans for me to succeed. I plan to succeed.*
> *I will succeed. As a child of God, I have a right to succeed.*
> *Everything I put my hands to, will prosper.*
> *God gives me creative ideas and witty inventions.*
> *God gives me good success.*

Joshua 1:8 says, "This book of the law shall not depart out of thy mouth; but thou shalt meditate therein day and night, that thou mayest observe to do according to all that is written therein: for then thou shalt make thy way prosperous, and then thou shalt have good success."

Psalm 1:1-3 says, "Blessed is the man that walketh not in the counsel of the ungodly, nor standeth in the way of sinners, nor sitteth in the seat of the scornful. But his delight is in the law of the Lord; and in his law doth he meditate day and night. And he shall be like a tree planted by the rivers of water, that bringeth forth his fruit in his season; his leaf also shall not wither; and whatsoever he doeth shall prosper."

Philippians 4:13 says, "I can do all things through Christ which strengtheneth me."

Philippians 3:13,14 says, "Brethren, I count not myself to have apprehended: but this one thing I do, forgetting those things which are behind, and reaching forth unto those things which are before, I press toward the mark for the prize of the high calling of God in Christ Jesus."

3 John 2 says, "Beloved, I wish above all things that thou mayest prosper and be in health, even as thy soul prospereth."

Remember, God wants us to succeed in life.

Iron *Sharpens* Iron

Study Notes

Additional Scripture References:
_____
_____
_____
_____
_____

Notes:
_____
_____
_____
_____
_____
_____
_____
_____
_____
_____
_____
_____
_____
_____
_____
_____
_____

Iron *Sharpens* Iron

A Life Of Abundance

Dear Friend:

God wants us to have abundance in every area of our lives. Abundance is *plenty,* and *overflowing blessings.* God wants us to have an abundance of wisdom, an abundance of success, an abundance of favor, and an abundance of prosperity. Have you ever been in a situation where you felt that you were going under, and just as you were about to hit rock bottom, God stepped in with abundant provision. Isn't that like God! He may not come when we think He should come, but He's always on time providing us with abundance.

In the fall of the year, my mother decorates her dinning room table with a "horn of plenty" centerpiece. This centerpiece has fruit, flowers, and ears of grains overflowing from it. All throughout the room, she displays a harvest motif, and whenever I look around the room, it reminds me of a bountiful harvest, abundance.

Whenever we look into the Word of God [the Bible], it should remind us that God is a God of abundance and He has a bountiful harvest for those who serve Him. Some of you may be saying, "I've been serving God for a long time and I haven't seen much abundance in my life!" My friend, we must have faith and confidence in God's Word. We must believe that He will bring abundance into our lives. If we believe God for abundance, it'll surely come.

Exodus 36:6,7 says, "And Moses gave commandment, and they caused it to be proclaimed throughout the camp, saying, Let neither man nor woman make any more work for the offering of the sanctuary. So the people were restrained from bringing. For the stuff they had was sufficient for all the work to make it, and too much."

Psalm 105:37 says, "He brought them forth also with silver and gold: and there was not one feeble person among their tribes."

Job 36:11 says, "If they obey and serve him, they shall spend their days in prosperity, and their years in pleasures."

Psalm 23:1,5 says, "The Lord is my shepherd; I shall not want. Thou preparest a table before me in the presence of mine enemies: thou anointest my head with oil; my cup runneth over."

Ephesians 3:20 says, "Now unto him that is able to do exceeding abundantly above all that we ask or think, according to the power that worketh in us."

Philippians 4:19 says, "But my God shall supply all your need according to his riches in glory by Christ Jesus."

3 John 2 says, "Beloved, I wish above all things that thou mayest prosper and be in health, even as thy soul prospereth."

Remember, God wants us to have a life of abundance.

Iron *Sharpens* Iron

Study Notes

Additional Scripture References:
_____
_____
_____
_____
_____

Notes:
_____
_____
_____
_____
_____
_____
_____
_____
_____
_____
_____
_____
_____
_____
_____

Iron *Sharpens* Iron

A Path Of Light

Dear Friend:

Jesus wants to illuminate our path. He wants to take us off of the crooked path and place our feet on a straight path. Jesus wants to pull us out of the ditch of darkness onto His marvelous path of light. He wants to shine light upon our way, so we can clearly see the wonderful things that He has placed for us on our path. If we walk the path that the Lord has illuminated for us, we will receive everything we need.

The first thing that God created, before He created the world and the things in the world, is light. (See Genesis chapter 1). And before anything can be created in our world, there must first be light. That light is *"the light of illumination"*, *"the light of understanding"*, *"the light of creativity"*, *"the light of revelation"*, *"the light of comprehension"*, and *"the light of cognition"*. The Lord wants to show us wealth and how to get it. He wants to show us health and how to obtain it. He wants to show us what to do and how to do it.

2 Samuel 22:29 says, "For thou art my lamp, O Lord: and the Lord will lighten my darkness."

Proverbs 4:18 says, "But the path of the just is as the shining light, that shineth more and more unto the perfect day."

Psalm 36:9 says, "For with thee is the fountain of life: in thy light shall we see light."

Psalm 37:23 says, "The steps of a good man are ordered by the Lord: and he delighteth in his way."

Psalm 32:8 says, "I will instruct thee and teach thee in the way which thou shalt go: I will guide thee with mine eye."

Ephesians 1:18 says, "The eyes of your understanding being enlightened; that ye may know what is the hope of his calling, and what the riches of the glory of his inheritance in the saints."

Psalm 119:105 says, "Thy word is a lamp unto my feet, and a light unto my path."

Isaiah 45:2,3 says, "I will go before thee, and make the crooked places straight: I will break in pieces the gates of brass, and cut in sunder the bars of iron: And I will give thee the treasures of darkness, and hidden riches of secret places, that thou mayest know that I, the Lord, which call thee by thy name, am the God of Israel."

Remember, we will receive everything we need, when we walk on the path of light.

Iron *Sharpens* Iron

Study Notes

Additional Scripture References:
_____
_____
_____
_____
_____
_____

Notes:
_____
_____
_____
_____
_____
_____
_____
_____
_____
_____
_____
_____
_____
_____
_____
_____

Iron *Sharpens* Iron

Working Our Faith

Dear Friend:

We hear so much about faith, and no matter how much we hear, our faith will not work for us, unless we put it to work. The Book of James tells us *"faith without works is dead"* (James 2:26). You know, dead faith never produces anything. This is why we must add life to our faith. We add life to our faith by doing something. Faith without corresponding action is dead. Faith is an action word, and if we desire to see results in our lives, we must back our faith up with action.

Have you ever seen an automobile without tires? It can't go places. It sits idly by, and if it continues to go without tires, it will eventually become rubbish. We shouldn't let our faith sit idly by and become rubbish. Putting action to our faith is like putting tires on an automobile. Our faith wants to take us places in life.

The devil will oppose our faith. He will not let us go through life without opposition. But we can rest assured that God is with us, He will not forsake us, and He will not fail us. This is why the Bible tells us to fight the good faith of faith (1 Timothy 6:12). The reason why it's a good fight is because the end result is victory. With God, we win all the time.

In Joshua chapter 1, God told Joshua to be strong and very courageous. That He will be with him everywhere he goes. God also told Joshua that if he does according to what was written in the Book of the law [this was the Bible in Joshua's day], that he will prosper and have good success. Joshua did according to what was written in the Book of the law, and he prospered and had good success. Joshua added action to his faith.

If we want to see victory as the end result of our faith, we must add action to our faith. We must do what God tells us to do.

Hebrews 11:8-11 says, "By faith Abraham, when he was called to go out into a place which he should after receive for an inheritance, obeyed; and he went out, not knowing whither he went. By faith he sojourned in the land of promise, as in a strange country, dwelling in tabernacles with Isaac and Jacob, the heirs with him of the same promise: For he looked for a city which hath foundations, whose builder and maker is God. Through faith also Sara herself received strength to conceive seed, and was delivered of a child when she was past age, because she judged him faithful who had promised."

Matthew 9:20-22 says, "And, behold, a woman, which was diseased with an issue of blood twelve years, came behind him, and touched the hem of his garment: For she said within herself, If I may but touch his garment, I shall be whole. But Jesus turned him about, and when he saw her, he said, Daughter, be of good comfort; thy faith hath made thee whole."

Remember, *"Faith without corresponding action is dead"*.

Iron *Sharpens* Iron

Study Notes

Additional Scripture References:
_____
_____
_____
_____
_____

Notes:
_____
_____
_____
_____
_____
_____
_____
_____
_____
_____
_____
_____
_____
_____
_____

Iron *Sharpens* Iron

The God Kind Of Love

Dear Friend:

Do you know that the Word of God [the Bible] has so much to say about love? Jesus gave us a new commandment, and that is the commandment of love. The commandment of love meets all the requirements and is the fulfilling of the Law (Romans 13:10 *The Amplified Bible*). What Paul was talking about in the Epistle of Romans, is the God kind of love. As Christians we should demonstrate the God kind of love, not only toward the Body of Christ but toward all men. Jesus said in John 13:35, "By this shall all men know that ye are my disciples, if ye have love one to another."

Love covers the multitude of sins (1 Peter 4:8 *The Amplified Bible*). Love does no wrong to his or her neighbor and it never hurts anybody (Romans 13:10 *The Amplified Bible*). So instead of us judging, criticizing, and putting others down, we should demonstrate love. We should put the love of God to work in our lives. If we want our prayers to work, we must make sure that we are demonstrating love. If we want our faith to work, we must make sure that we are demonstrating love. Some of you may be saying, "I've tried to demonstrate love, but I am having a hard time demonstrating love toward those who are not so loveable". Well the remedy is 1 Corinthians 13.

Let's confess *The Amplified Bible* version of 1 Corinthians 13:4-8:

> *Love endures long and is patient and kind; love never is envious nor boils over with jealous, is not boastful or vainglorious, does not display itself haughtily.*
>
> *It is not conceited (arrogant and inflated with pride); it is not rude (unmannerly) and does not act unbecomingly. Love (God's love in us) does not insist on it's own rights or its own way, for it is not self-seeking; it is not touchy or fretful or resentful; it takes no account of the evil done to it [it pays no attention to a suffered wrong].*
>
> *It does not rejoice at injustice and unrighteousness, but rejoices when right and truth prevail. Love bears up under anything and everything that comes, is ever ready to believe the best of every person, its hopes are fadeless under all circumstances, and it endures everything [without weakening]. Love never fails [never fades out or becomes obsolete or comes to an end].*

As we continue to confess 1 Corinthians 13:4-8, it will become easier for us to love those who are not so loveable. The Word of God tells us to love our enemies, bless them that curse us, do good to them that hate us, and to pray for those who despitefully use us and persecute us (Matthew 5:44). The Word of God also tells us that God is love and he that dwells in love dwells in God and God in him (1 John 4:16).

Remember, we must demonstrate the God kind of love toward everyone.

Iron *Sharpens* Iron

Study Notes

Additional Scripture References:
___

Notes:
___

Iron *Sharpens* Iron

What Are You Thinking?

Dear Friend:

What are you thinking? Are you thinking on good things, or are you thinking on bad things? Are you thinking that you'll never be a success, or are you thinking that with God's supernatural ability, you can always be a success? Are you thinking bad things about others, or are you thinking good things about others? Do you think good things about yourself, or do you think bad things about yourself?

We should think on what the Word of God [the Bible] tells us to think on and as Christians, we should think good things about others and ourselves. Philippians 4:8 says, "Finally, brethren, whatsoever things are true, whatsoever things are honest, whatsoever things are just, whatsoever things are pure, whatsoever things are lovely, whatsoever things are of good report; if there be any virtue, and if there be any praise, think on these things."

Proverbs 23:7 says, "For as he thinketh in his heart, so is he." Do you know that we become the product of what we constantly think and feed our minds upon, whether it is bad or good? We can be a success in life or a failure in life by what we constantly think and feed our minds upon. That is why the Word of God tells us to renew our minds. Romans 12:2 says, "And be not conformed to this world: but be ye transformed by the renewing of your mind, that ye may prove what is that good, and acceptable, and perfect, will of God." In order to think on good things, we must continue to renew our minds with the Word of God on a daily basis.

Ephesians 4:23 says, "And be renewed in the spirit of your mind."

2 Corinthians 10:5 says, "Casting down imaginations, and every high thing that exalteth itself against the knowledge of God, and bringing into captivity every thought to the obedience of Christ."

Colossians 3:2 says, "Set your affection [mind] on things above, not on things on the earth."

Philippians 2:5 says, "Let this mind be in you, which was also in Christ Jesus."

Isaiah 26:3 says, "Thou wilt keep him in perfect peace, whose mind is stayed on thee: because he trusteth in thee."

Colossians 1:21,22 says, "And you, that were sometime alienated and enemies in your mind by wicked works, yet now hath he reconciled In the body of his flesh through death, to present you holy and unblameable and unreproveable in his sight."

1 Peter 1:13 says, "Wherefore gird up the loins of your mind, be sober, and hope to the end for the grace that is to be brought unto you at the revelation of Jesus Christ."

Remember, we should think good things about others and ourselves.

Iron *Sharpens* Iron

Study Notes

Additional Scripture References:

_____
_____
_____
_____
_____

Notes:

_____
_____
_____
_____
_____
_____
_____
_____
_____
_____
_____
_____
_____
_____
_____
_____
_____

Iron *Sharpens* Iron

Divine Love

Dear Friend:

Do you know that we have divine love living on the inside of us? The Bible tells us that God poured out His love in our hearts by the Holy Ghost. Romans 5:5 says, ". . . The love of God is shed abroad in our hearts by the Holy Ghost, which is given unto us." When we became born-again, God placed everything that we need inside of us to love.

The Bible tells us that God is love. The essence of God is love, and if we are children of God, then we have the nature of God in us, which is love.

Have you ever watched small children? They are imitators of their parents. They say whatever they hear their parents say, and they do whatever they see their parents do. We are children of a love God; therefore we should be imitators of our Heavenly Father.

Divine love doesn't envy others. It rejoices when others are blessed. Divine love doesn't talk about others. It prays for others. Divine love isn't superficial or pretentious. It is pure. Divine love doesn't mistreat people. It treats people the way it wants to be treated. Divine love isn't selfish. It gives. Divine love doesn't covet. It is thankful for what it has. Divine love doesn't hurt. It heals. Divine love isn't impatient with others. It takes time with others. Divine love doesn't curse others. It blesses others. Divine love doesn't hate. It loves.

John 3:16 says, "For God so loved the world, that he gave his only begotten Son, that whosoever believeth in him should not perish, but have everlasting life."

1 John 4:7,8 says, "Beloved, let us love one another: for love is of God; and every one that loveth is born of God, and knoweth God. He that loveth not knoweth not God; for God is love."

Romans 13:10 says, "Love worketh no ill to his neighbour; therefore love is the fulfilling of the law."

1 Peter 1:22 says, "Seeing ye have purified your souls in obeying the truth through the Spirit unto unfeigned love of the brethren, see that ye love one another with a pure heart fervently."

Galatians 5:22,23 says, "But the fruit of the Spirit is love, joy, peace, longsuffering, gentleness, goodness, faith, Meekness, temperance: against such there is no law."

Matthew 5:44 says, "But I say unto you, Love your enemies, bless them that curse you, do good to them that hate you, and pray for them which despitefully use you, and persecute you."

1 John 3:18 says, "My little children, let us not love in word, neither in tongue; but in deed and in truth."

Remember to let that divine love on the inside work on the outside.

Iron *Sharpens* Iron

Study Notes

Additional Scripture References:

Notes:

Iron *Sharpens* Iron

The Fruit Of Our Labor

Dear Friend:

The Bible tells us that God will bless the fruit of our labor. Deuteronomy 28:8,12 says, "The Lord shall command the blessing upon thee in thy storehouses, and in all that thou settest thine hand unto. The Lord shall open unto thee his good treasure, the heaven to give the rain unto thy land in his season, and to bless all the work of thine hand."

Some of us have wondered why we are not prospering? Some of us are not prospering, because we haven't put our hands to anything. We haven't made any effort to work. Some of us are just sitting around waiting for someone to come along and bless us. We are waiting for our *"ship"* to come in. Most likely our ship will never come in. We must get up and do something. We must put forth an effort to work. God will prosper our efforts.

Some people don't want to work. As a matter of fact, they have so many excuses why they shouldn't work. But the Bible tells us that if we don't work, we shouldn't eat. 2 Thessalonians 3:10 says, ". . . That if any would not work, neither should he eat." If we don't work, we continue to lead our families and ourselves into poverty, and poverty is a curse. Laziness will lead to poverty, but honest work will lead to prosperity.

Have you ever heard that an idle mind is the devil's workshop? An idle mind will cause us to become discontent, busybodies, always gossiping, and getting into the affairs of others. If we are working, we don't have time to gossip. We don't have time to get into the affairs of others.

As Christians, we should not be freeloaders in life. We should earn our keep. We should not slack off in doing our duty, that is, providing for our family and ourselves.

2 Thessalonians 3:10 says, "For even when we were with you, this we commanded you, that if any would not work, neither should he eat."

Proverbs 21:25 says, "The desire of the slothful killeth him; for his hands refuse to labour."

Ephesians 4:28 says, "Let him that stole steal no more: but rather let him labour, working with his hands the thing which is good, that he may have to give to him that needeth."

Proverbs 6:6-11 says, "Go to the ant, thou sluggard; consider her ways, and be wise: Which having no guide, overseer, or ruler, Provideth her meat in the summer, and gathereth her food in the harvest. How long wilt thou sleep, O sluggard? when wilt thou arise out of thy sleep? Yet a little sleep, a little slumber, a little folding of the hands to sleep: So shall thy poverty come as one that travelleth, and thy want as an armed man."

Remember, laziness will lead to poverty, but honest work will lead to prosperity.

Iron *Sharpens* Iron

Study Notes

Additional Scripture References:
___
___
___
___
___

Notes:
___
___
___
___
___
___
___
___
___
___
___
___
___
___
___
___
___

Iron *Sharpens* Iron

Be A Person Of Your Word

Dear Friend:

Some of us have good intentions when we make commitments and promises to others. It is hard for some of us to say *"No",* when we know that we are already over committed, or can't fulfill a promise. Even though our intentions are good, we should only make commitments and promises that we plan to keep. Psalm 15:4 says, ". . . He [the Lord] honoureth them that fear the Lord. He that sweareth to his own hurt, and changeth not." This verse means that we should keep our commitment or promise even if it hurts us to keep it.

It is best for us not to make a promise or a commitment, if we don't plan to keep it, because a person is known by the integrity of his [or her] word. James 1:8 says, "A double minded man [or woman] is unstable in all his [or her] ways." "Unstable" means *not reliable*, *not dependable*, *not loyal*, *not faithful*, and *not trustworthy*.

In the past, men made promises and commitments with a handshake. This handshake was like signing their name on a written legal contract. They believed in their word. They kept their word. Their word was their bond. The older generation was known by the integrity of their word. As Christians, we should keep our word. We should be known by the integrity of our word.

If we are not a person of our word, it is hard for us to trust and believe God. It is hard for us to believe the promises and blessings that God has provided for us in His Word [the Bible]. Numbers 23:19 says, "God is not a man, that he should lie; neither the son of man, that he should repent: hath he said, and shall he not do it? or hath he spoken, and shall he not make it good?"

As children of God, let us purpose in our hearts to keep our promises and commitments that we make to others. Let's imitate our Heavenly Father by keeping our promises and commitments.

Proverbs 11:3 says, "The integrity of the upright shall guide them: but the perverseness of transgressors shall destroy them."

Psalm 15:4 says, "In whose eyes a vile person is contemned; but he honoureth them that fear the Lord. He that sweareth to his own hurt, and changeth not."

James 1:8 says, "A double minded man is unstable in all his ways."

Proverbs 20:7 says, "The just man walketh in his integrity: his children are blessed after him."

Proverbs 19:1 says, "Better is the poor that walketh in his integrity, than he that is perverse in his lips, and is a fool."

Remember, our word should be our bond.

Iron *Sharpens* Iron

Study Notes

Additional Scripture References:
_____
_____
_____
_____
_____
_____

Notes:
_____
_____
_____
_____
_____
_____
_____
_____
_____
_____
_____
_____
_____
_____
_____
_____
_____

Iron *Sharpens* Iron

Iron *Sharpens* Iron

Is Christ In Your Christmas?

Dear Friend:

The world has taken Christ out of Christmas. They have substituted "Xmas" for "Christmas". But as Christian, we should put *"Christ"* back into Christmas. What I mean is, that we should exemplify Christ this Christmas to our loved ones, and to all those we come in contact with.

The following are a few things of what "Xmas" means to the world:
- *Wish to have more money to buy more expensive gifts*
- *Rush and run around in a frenzy to buy as much as they can*
- *Think not about lending a helping hand to someone who's in need*
- *Attend as many parties and social events that they can*
- *Worry, feel depressed, and frustrated*
- *Drink, eat, and drink some more*

The following are a few things of what "Christmas" should mean to the Christian:
- *Tell someone about Jesus*
- *Praise and worship the Lord for who He is*
- *Lend a helping hand to someone who's in need*
- *Give a word of encouragement to those around us*
- *Spend time with family and loved ones*
- *Visit the elderly or someone who may be lonely*

Isaiah 9:6 says, "For unto us a child is born, unto us a son is given: and the government shall be upon his shoulder: and his name shall be called Wonderful, Counsellor, The mighty God, The everlasting Father, The Prince of Peace."

Isaiah 7:13,14 says, "And he said, Hear ye now, O house of David; Is it a small thing for you to weary men, but will ye weary my God also? Therefore the Lord himself shall give you a sign; Behold, a virgin shall conceive, and bear a son, and shall call his name Immanuel."

Luke 2:8-11 says, "And there were in the same country shepherds abiding in the field, keeping watch over their flock by night. And, lo, the angel of the Lord came upon them, and the glory of the Lord shone round about them: and they were sore afraid. And the angel said unto them, Fear not: for, behold, I bring you good tidings of great joy, which shall be to all people. For unto you is born this day in the city of David a Saviour, which is Christ the Lord."

Matthew 1:21-23 says, "And she shall bring forth a son, and thou shalt call his name Jesus: for he shall save his people from their sins. Now all this was done, that it might be fulfilled which was spoken of the Lord by the prophet, saying, Behold, a virgin shall be with child, and shall bring forth a son, and they shall call his name Emmanuel, which being interpreted is, God with us."

Remember to put *"Christ"* back into Christmas.

Iron *Sharpens* Iron

Study Notes

Additional Scripture References:

Notes:

Iron *Sharpens* Iron

Blessed!

Dear Friend:

Deuteronomy 28:1-13 tells us about the many blessings in obeying God and following His commandments. Following is my modern day interpretation of some of these Scriptures:

All these blessings will come upon us and accompany and overtake us, if we walk in obedience to the commands of the Lord. We will be blessed in the city and blessed in the country. Our children will be blessed and our families will be blessed. Our businesses will increase and prosper.

Our pantries and refrigerators will be blessed. We'll be blessed in the grocery stores and blessed in the shopping malls. We'll be blessed when we leave our homes and we'll be blessed when we return to our homes. The enemies that rise up against us will be defeated before us. They will come at us from one direction, but they'll run in terror from us in seven directions.

The Lord will command blessings upon our bank accounts, investments, and purses. The Lord will bless us on our jobs, and everything that we put our hands to will be blessed.

All the people on earth will see that the Lord has commanded blessings upon us, and they will fear us, and be envious and jealous of us. The Lord will give us the power to prosper. We will lend to many, and not borrow from anyone. We will always be at the top, and never at the bottom.

Deuteronomy 28:2-6 says, "And all these blessings shall come on thee, and overtake thee, if thou shalt hearken unto the voice of the Lord thy God. Blessed shalt thou be in the city, and blessed shalt thou be in the field. Blessed shall be the fruit of thy body, and the fruit of thy ground, and the fruit of thy cattle, the increase of thy kine, and the flocks of thy sheep. Blessed shall be thy basket and thy store. Blessed shalt thou be when thou comest in, and blessed shalt thou be when thou goest out."

Psalm 67:6 says, "Then shall the earth yield her increase; and God, even our own God, shall bless us."

Job 36:11 says, "If they obey and serve him, they shall spend their days in prosperity, and their years in pleasures."

Ephesians 1:3 says, "Blessed be the God and Father of our Lord Jesus Christ, who hath blessed us with all spiritual blessings in heavenly places in Christ."

Psalm 112:3 says, "Wealth and riches shall be in his house: and his righteousness endureth for ever."

Remember, we are *blessed!*

Iron *Sharpens* Iron

Study Notes

Additional Scripture References:

Notes:

Iron *Sharpens* Iron

We Don't Have To Fear

Dear Friend:

Many of us have experienced fear one time or another in our lives, and some of us may be still experiencing fear. What is fear? Fear is *"the opposite of faith"*. Fear is *"faith in the devil and his works"*. The devil often brings fear to try and make the Word of God [the Bible] null and ineffective in our lives. He wants us to believe that the Word is powerless. But to the contrary, God's Word is *POWERFUL* and it can handle anything that the devil may try and bring our way.

When we are overcome by fear, we can't think right, we lose control of our emotions, and we say and do things without first thinking it out. When we are in fear, it's hard for us to make right decisions. Sometimes it's hard for us to make any decisions. We shouldn't allow fear to overtake us, because fear brings torment, confusion, suffering, and bondage. There are so many people who have many different fears: fear of flying, fear of being rejected, fear of failure, fear of change, fear of being alone, fear of man, and I can go on, but God doesn't want us to live in fear. 2 Timothy 1:7 tells us that God has not given us the spirit of fear.

God tells us so many times in His Word not to fear, because He is with us and He will help us (Isaiah 41:13). Whenever fear tries to come and attach itself to us, we need to resist it with the Word of God. Jesus lives in us and He is greater than any fear. Greater is He [Jesus] who is in us than he [the devil] who is in the world (1 John 4:4). We don't have to fear, because Jesus gave us victory over fear.

Proverbs 3:24-26 says, "When thou liest down, thou shalt not be afraid: yea, thou shalt lie down, and thy sleep shall be sweet. Be not afraid of sudden fear, neither of the desolation of the wicked, when it cometh. For the Lord shall be thy confidence, and shall keep thy foot from being taken."

Hebrews 13:6 says, "So that we may boldly say, The Lord is my helper, and I will not fear what man shall do unto me."

1 John 4:18 says, "There is no fear in love; but perfect love casteth out fear: because fear hath torment. He that feareth is not made perfect in love."

Psalm 91:5-7 says, "Thou shalt not be afraid for the terror by night; nor for the arrow that flieth by day; Nor for the pestilence that walketh in darkness; nor for the destruction that wasteth at noonday. A thousand shall fall at thy side, and ten thousand at thy right hand; but it shall not come nigh thee."

2 Timothy 1:7 says, "For God hath not given us the spirit of fear; but of power, and of love, and of a sound mind."

Remember, God wants us to live in faith, and not live in fear.

Iron *Sharpens* Iron

Study Notes

Additional Scripture References:

Notes:

Iron *Sharpens* Iron

We Serve The Mighty God

Dear Friend:

Do you know we serve the mighty God? We can see by the majestic mountain ranges, the roaring waterfalls and the spectacular canyons that God is mighty. We can see by the thousands of stars in the sky and the roaring oceans that God is mighty. The Vines Expository Dictionary defines "mighty" as "*power, ability to do anything*". Isn't this just like the God that we serve! He has the power and the ability to do anything. We must believe that God has the power and the ability to do all things good in our lives.

You've heard about the many powers in the world; corporate power, political power, nuclear power, and rocket power, just to name a few. None of these powers can compare to the *MIGHTY* power of God. Ephesians 1:19 in *The Amplified Bible* says, "And [so that you can know and understand] what is the immeasurable and unlimited and surpassing greatness of His power in and for us who believe, as demonstrated in the working of His mighty strength." This mighty power is the same power that raised Jesus from the dead. I call it *resurrection* power and that's some power.

David operated in the mighty power of God. In 1 Samuel 16:13, Samuel took the horn of oil and anointed David and from that day on, the Spirit of the Lord came upon David in power. The power that David was anointed with was the mighty power of God. It was the same power that allowed David to defeat Goliath and win the battle for Israel.

I want the real power, that *MIGHTY* power of God to operate in my life. How about you?

Ephesians 1:19 says, "And what is the exceeding greatness of his power to us-ward who believe, according to the working of his mighty power."

Psalm 24:8 says, "Who is this King of glory? The Lord strong and mighty, the Lord mighty in battle."

Zephaniah 3:17 says, "The Lord thy God in the midst of thee is mighty; he will save, he will rejoice over thee with joy; he will rest in his love, he will joy over thee with singing."

2 Corinthians 10:4 says, "For the weapons of our warfare are not carnal, but mighty through God to the pulling down of strong holds."

Ephesians 6:10 says, "Finally, my brethren, be strong in the Lord, and in the power of his might."

Exodus 15:6 says, "Thy right hand, O Lord, is become glorious in power: thy right hand, O Lord, hath dashed in pieces the enemy."

Remember, we serve the *"MIGHTY"* God.

Iron *Sharpens* Iron

Study Notes

Additional Scripture References:
_____
_____
_____
_____
_____
_____

Notes:
_____
_____
_____
_____
_____
_____
_____
_____
_____
_____
_____
_____
_____
_____
_____
_____
_____
_____
_____

Iron *Sharpens* Iron

Benefits

Dear Friend:

We've heard about the different benefit packages. There are health benefits that we receive when we work for different companies. There are investment benefits that we receive when we participate in the company's IRA or 401K programs.

There are benefits we receive when we exercise and eat the right kinds of food, and there are benefits when we go to school to learn a trade or a profession. Even though those benefits are good, they can't compare to the benefits of God. God's Word [the Bible] tells us that He provides us daily with benefits (Psalm 68:19). You might ask, "What are some of the benefits of God?" I'll just list a few:

1. *He has provided healing for us through Jesus (Matthew 8:17).*
2. *He made us heirs and joint heirs with Christ (Romans 8:16,17).*
3. *He made us more than conquerors (Romans 8:37).*
4. *He made us righteous (2 Corinthians 5:21).*
5. *He has made us accepted in the Beloved (Ephesians 1:6).*
6. *He made provisions for us (Philippians 4:19).*
7. *He made us ambassadors (2 Corinthians 5:20).*
8. *He has given us power and authority over the devil (Luke 10:19).*
9. *He has given us eternal life through Jesus Christ (1 John 5:11).*

I can go on, but there's no way that I can include all of the benefits of God in this letter. All of the benefits of God are for us and as children of God, He wants us to enjoy them all.

Psalm 68:19 says, "Blessed be the Lord, who daily loadeth us with benefits, even the God of our salvation."

Psalm 103:2-5 says, "Bless the Lord, O my soul, and forget not all his benefits: Who forgiveth all thine iniquities; who healeth all thy diseases; Who redeemeth thy life from destruction; who crowneth thee with lovingkindness and tender mercies; Who satisfieth thy mouth with good things; so that thy youth is renewed like the eagle's."

Psalm 116:12-14 says, "What shall I render unto the Lord for all his benefits toward me? I will take the cup of salvation, and call upon the name of the Lord. I will pay my vows unto the Lord now in the presence of all his people."

Remember, God benefits are for us, and He wants us to enjoy them *all*.

Iron *Sharpens* Iron

Study Notes

Additional Scripture References:
_____
_____
_____
_____
_____
_____

Notes:
_____
_____
_____
_____
_____
_____
_____
_____
_____
_____
_____
_____
_____
_____
_____
_____
_____

Iron *Sharpens* Iron

Iron *Sharpens* Iron

Worship God

Dear Friend:

We spend most of our time in prayer asking God to bless us, and to give us this, and to give us that. Instead of constantly asking God to bless us, we should take some time out to worship Him. Some of you might be saying, "I don't really know how to worship God, I don't know what to say". Well, worship is simply giving reverence [honor] to God. The Word [the Bible] admonishes us to worship the Lord God our Maker (Psalm 95:6). The Word also admonishes us to give glory that is due to His name and worship Him in the beauty of holiness (1 Chronicles 16:29).

As we get into the Word and find out more about God, we will come to realize that God is majestic, awesome, and more than wonderful. Our minds can't comprehend all of the attributes of God. This is when we should stop and take some time to worship Him.

I've list a few Scriptures to help us with our worship to God:

1. *Worship God because He is holy (Psalm 99:9).*
2. *Worship God because He is faithful (Hebrews 10:23, 1 Corinthians 1:9).*
3. *Worship God because He is the Creator (Isaiah 42:5, Isaiah 45:18).*
4. *Worship God because He is greater than all (John 10:29).*
5. *Worship God because He is mighty (Zephaniah 3:17).*
6. *Worship God because He is good (Psalm 34:8, Psalm 119:68).*
7. *Worship God because He is merciful (Psalm 116:5).*
8. *Worship God because He is righteous (Daniel 9:14, Psalm 145:17).*

Instead of seeking God's hand, we should seek His face. We should get into His presence and worship Him. As we worship God, we will become more aware of His presence.

John 4:24 says, "God is a Spirit: and they that worship him must worship him in spirit and in truth."

Psalm 29:2 says, "Give unto the Lord the glory due unto his name; worship the Lord in the beauty of holiness."

Revelation 14:7 says, "Saying with a loud voice, Fear God, and give glory to him; for the hour of his judgment is come: and worship him that made heaven, and earth, and the sea, and the fountains of waters."

1 Chronicles 29:11,12 says, "Thine, O Lord, is the greatness, and the power, and the glory, and the victory, and the majesty: for all that is in the heaven and in the earth is thine; thine is the kingdom, O Lord, and thou art exalted as head above all. Both riches and honour come of thee, and thou reignest over all; and in thine hand is power and might; and in thine hand it is to make great, and to give strength unto all."

Remember, we should worship God for *who* He is.

Iron *Sharpens* Iron

Study Notes

Additional Scripture References:
_____
_____
_____
_____
_____
_____

Notes:
_____
_____
_____
_____
_____
_____
_____
_____
_____
_____
_____
_____
_____
_____
_____
_____
_____

Iron *Sharpens* Iron

God Is Our Source

Dear Friend:

All throughout the Word of God [the Bible], we see how God provided for His people over and over again. We see how He provided food for Elijah the prophet (1 Kings 17 chapter). We also see how He provided provision for the children of Israel in the wilderness (Exodus 16 chapter). When Jesus and the disciples needed money to pay their taxes, God provided money through the mouth of a fish (Matthew 17 chapter).

The Word of God shows us that God is the source of His people, and He wants to be our source. God wants to supply all of our needs. If we are living according to the Word of God, we don't have to worry about going with our needs unmet. Philippians 4:19 tells us that God shall supply all of our needs according to His riches in glory through Christ Jesus. God will not only supply all of our needs, but He'll supply our wants.

As children of God, we shouldn't be in want for food and we shouldn't be in want for clothes. We shouldn't be in want for anything. Psalm 23:1 tells us that the Lord is our shepherd and we shall not want. As children of God, we should be eating the good of the land, wearing the good of the land, and living in the good of the land. Isaiah 1:19 tells us that if we are willing and obedient [to do what God tells us to do], we shall eat the good of the land.

We should look to God, who is our source to bring us opportunities and open doors for us. We should look to God, who is our source to provide all of our needs. We should look to God, who is our source to make all things good in our lives. We shouldn't look to man as our source, but look to God, because He is a better provider than we can ever dream of someone else being for us. God wants to bless us, and He wants to meet all of our needs.

Psalm 37:25 says, "I have been young, and now am old; yet have I not seen the righteous forsaken, nor his seed begging bread."

Luke 12:24-31 says, "Consider the ravens: for they neither sow nor reap; which neither have storehouse nor barn; and God feedeth them: how much more are ye better than the fowls? And which of you with taking thought can add to his stature one cubit? If ye then be not able to do that thing which is least, why take ye thought for the rest? Consider the lilies how they grow: they toil not, they spin not; and yet I say unto you, that Solomon in all his glory was not arrayed like one of these. If then God so clothe the grass, which is to day in the field, and to morrow is cast into the oven; how much more will he clothe you, O ye of little faith? And seek not ye what ye shall eat, or what ye shall drink, neither be ye of doubtful mind. For all these things do the nations of the world seek after: and your Father knoweth that ye have need of these things. But rather seek ye the kingdom of God; and all these things shall be added unto you."

Remember, God wants to meet all of our needs.

Iron *Sharpens* Iron

Study Notes

Additional Scripture References:

Notes:

Iron *Sharpens* Iron

A Good Work

Dear Friend:

God wants to work a good work in us. But before God can work a good work in us, He must first work some things out of us. Sometimes God allows situations to come into our lives to perfect us.

Have you ever stood in a check out line at the grocery store, and a customer ahead of you causes the line to be held up for a price check? Have you ever flown on an airplane and a couple with a baby is seated right behind you, and the baby is irritable throughout the entire flight? It could be that God is working impatience and insensitivity out of us so that He can work patience and sensitivity to others in us.

The Book of James tells us to let patience have full play and do a thorough work, that we may be fully developed and lacking in nothing (James 1:4).

Has someone ever rubbed you the wrong way? We may be rough around the edges and this someone is as sandpaper to help smooth off our rough edges. Have you tried to avoid or get around situations that you encounter? We must face those situations head on and conquer them. Have things in your life didn't work out like you thought they should? We shouldn't become discourage. God is changing our hearts and expanding our horizons. God is aligning us for greater blessings.

Philippians 2:13 says, "For it is God which worketh in you both to will and to do of his good pleasure."

Romans 8:28 says, "And we know that all things work together for good to them that love God, to them who are the called according to his purpose."

James 1:2-4 says, "My brethren, count it all joy when ye fall into divers temptations; Knowing this, that the trying of your faith worketh patience. But let patience have her perfect work, that ye may be perfect and entire, wanting nothing."

Proverbs 27:17 says, "Iron sharpeneth iron; so a man sharpeneth the countenance of his friend."

2 Corinthians 9:8 says, "And God is able to make all grace abound toward you; that ye, always having all sufficiency in all things, may abound to every good work."

Philippians 1:6 says, "Being confident of this very thing, that he which hath begun a good work in you will perform it until the day of Jesus Christ."

Remember, God wants to work a good work in us and through us.

Iron *Sharpens* Iron

Study Notes

Additional Scripture References:

Notes:

Iron *Sharpens* Iron

Living A Long Life

Dear Friend:

God wants us to live a long and fruitful life upon the earth. God has promised us long life and He wants us to have a long and satisfying life. In other words, God wants us to live until we're satisfied. But in order for us to enjoy a long life, we must follow the instructions from the Word of God [the Bible]. We must keep the Word of God in our hearts and never let go of it (Proverbs 3:1 The Living Bible).

If we want to have a long life and *WELL* days upon the earth, we must honor our mother and father (Ephesians 6:2,3). "Honor" means *to respect and highly esteem*. Some of you may be saying, "My mother and father are deceased and I did not honor them like I should've when they were living". Well, just ask the Lord to forgive you [and He will], and go on with your life living for Him. Others of you may be saying, "My mother and father do not live like Christians". You must still honor them, because the Word of God tells us to honor them.

God will command blessings upon our lives for obeying His Word. We will not only have long life, but we will have prosperity along with it (Proverbs 3:1,2 NIV). God wants us to enjoy a long and satisfying life.

Proverbs 3:1,2 says, "My son, forget not my law; but let thine heart keep my commandments: For length of days, and long life, and peace, shall they add to thee."

Deuteronomy 5:33 says, "Ye shall walk in all the ways which the Lord your God hath commanded you, that ye may live, and that it may be well with you, and that ye may prolong your days in the land which ye shall possess."

Isaiah 38:1-5 says, "In those days was Hezekiah sick unto death. And Isaiah the prophet the son of Amoz came unto him, and said unto him, Thus saith the Lord, Set thine house in order: for thou shalt die, and not live. Then Hezekiah turned his face toward the wall, and prayed unto the Lord, And said, Remember now, O Lord, I beseech thee, how I have walked before thee in truth and with a perfect heart, and have done that which is good in thy sight. And Hezekiah wept sore. Then came the word of the Lord to Isaiah, saying, Go, and say to Hezekiah, Thus saith the Lord, the God of David thy father, I have heard thy prayer, I have seen thy tears: behold, I will add unto thy days fifteen years."

Proverbs 9:11 says, "For by me thy days shall be multiplied, and the years of thy life shall be increased."

Psalm 91:1,16 says, "He that dwelleth in the secret place of the most High shall abide under the shadow of the Almighty. With long life will I satisfy him, and show him my salvation."

Remember, God wants us to live a long and satisfying life.

Iron *Sharpens* Iron

Study Notes

Additional Scripture References:
_____
_____
_____
_____
_____

Notes:
_____
_____
_____
_____
_____
_____
_____
_____
_____
_____
_____
_____
_____
_____
_____
_____
_____
_____

Iron *Sharpens* Iron

Doing Impossible Things

Dear Friend:

Do you know that the God who can do the impossible, lives on the inside of us? If God lives on the inside of us, then we too can do impossible things. Believe God. Believe His Word [the Bible]. Believe in yourself, and you will be able to do things in your life you never thought were possible.

We were created to do extraordinary things in life. God did not create us to live a mundane life, sitting around hoping that things will change, and hoping one day that our lives will get better. God has anointed us to change things in our lives. He has placed everything in us to be a success.

As Christians, we should be operating on a higher level than the world. The world should look and marvel at us, because they don't understand how we can be so successful in life. We have greater resources than the world, because we have the Bible as our resource book. We have better instructions than the world, because we have the Bible as our instruction manual. We have superior wisdom than the world, because the Bible teaches us and guides us through life.

In Numbers chapters 13 and 14, God promised Moses to give the children of Israel a land that flowed with milk and honey, but they would have to go in and posses the land. So Moses sent out twelve spies to check out the land. Ten spies came back with an evil report. What they saw in the land intimidated them. They saw the people in the land as giants, and themselves as grasshoppers. They saw themselves defeated, which caused them to never enter into the land and enjoy it. But Joshua and Caleb were different, because they believed the God who can do impossible things. They came back with a good report. Joshua and Caleb saw themselves conquering and possessing the land, and they did. They entered in and enjoyed all the benefits of the land.

Joshua and Caleb should be our example (see the Book of Joshua). Whenever we are faced with what may seem impossible, we should remember that God has made us to do impossible things. God wants us to conquer and possess our promised land, and enjoy all it's benefits.

Philippians 4:13 says, "I can do all things through Christ which strengtheneth me."

1 John 4:4 says, "Ye are of God, little children, and have overcome them: because greater is he that is in you, than he that is in the world."

Romans 8:37 says, "Nay, in all these things we are more than conquerors through him that loved us."

Mark 9:23 says, "Jesus said unto him, If thou canst believe, all things are possible to him that believeth."

Remember, we were created to do impossible things.

Iron *Sharpens* Iron

Study Notes

Additional Scripture References:

Notes:

Iron *Sharpens* Iron

The Favor Of God

Dear Friend:

Some people work and struggle most of their lives to try to accomplish what can be accomplished in one day with the favor of God. The favor of God is *special privileges*, *an advantage*, and *preferential treatment*. God wants us to have favor operating in our lives. We should begin to declare God's favor upon our lives. We should expect people to be good to us. We should expect people to do good things for us.

When a person is born in a rich family, they are treated differently than the average person. They experience special privileges and advantages. We are born in the family of God, so we should expect people to help us and give us preferential treatment.

God wants us to become favor-inside minded. We shouldn't speak negative and defeated words over our lives. We should stop expecting to get the short end of the stick or barely get along. God wants us to have favor everywhere we go, and in everything that we do. With the favor of God operating in our lives, God will allow us to be in the right place at the right time. Favor will cause people to do something good for us.

Some of us may feel that we don't deserve the favor of God, because of our past sins. David did some bad things in his life, but David repented and God forgave him, and the Bible tells us that David was a man after God's own heart (see Psalm 51 chapter, 2 Samuel 12 chapter, and Acts 13:22).

Many of us may have situations that seem impossible, and some of us may be experiencing something bad in our lives. But if we begin to declare the favor of God upon our lives, our situation will change. God's favor will come to us and turn our situation around. With God's favor, doors will open for us. The Bible tells us that God opens doors that no man can shut (Revelation 3:8).

Job was in what seemed to be a hopeless situation, but when Job declared the favor of God upon his life, his situation was changed within one year. And God give Job twice as much as he had before (see Job 42 chapter).

Deuteronomy 28:2-6 says, "And all these blessings shall come on thee, and overtake thee, if thou shalt hearken unto the voice of the Lord thy God. Blessed shalt thou be in the city, and blessed shalt thou be in the field. Blessed shall be the fruit of thy body, and the fruit of thy ground, and the fruit of thy cattle, the increase of thy kine, and the flocks of thy sheep. Blessed shall be thy basket and thy store. Blessed shalt thou be when thou comest in, and blessed shalt thou be when thou goest out."

Psalm 23:6 says, "Surely goodness and mercy shall follow me all the days of my life: and I will dwell in the house of the Lord for ever."

Remember, we must declare and expect the favor of God to work in our lives.

Iron *Sharpens* Iron

Study Notes

Additional Scripture References:

Notes:

Iron *Sharpens* Iron

Just Do Good

Dear Friend:

Jesus did good everywhere He went. He once attended a wedding and when the wine ran out, He turned water into wine (John 2:1-3,8-10). Jesus went to Jarius' house and raised his little girl from the dead (Luke 8:41,42,51-55). He even raised Lazarus from the dead after he was buried for several days (see John 11 chapter). All throughout the Gospels (Matthew, Mark, Luke, and John), we see Jesus doing good everywhere He went. Acts 10:38 says, "How God anointed Jesus of Nazareth with the Holy Ghost and with power: who went about doing good, and healing all that were oppressed by the devil; for God was with him."

As Christians, we should follow Jesus' example by doing good. We should do good to our family and others. Some of us may be having a hard time doing good to others, we should just do it as unto the Lord. Luke 6:27,28,31 says, "But I say unto you which hear, Love your enemies, do good to them which hate you, Bless them that curse you, and pray for them which despitefully use you. And as ye would that men should do to you, do ye also to them likewise."

If we want God's bountiful blessings to be upon our lives, we must do good. When we do good to others, good will come back to us.

Psalm 125:4 says, "Do good, O Lord, unto those that be good, and to them that are upright in their hearts."

Galatians 5:13 says, "For, brethren, ye have been called unto liberty; only use not liberty for an occasion to the flesh, but by love serve one another."

Matthew 5:44 says, "But I say unto you, Love your enemies, bless them that curse you, do good to them that hate you, and pray for them which despitefully use you, and persecute you."

Galatians 6:7 says, "Be not deceived; God is not mocked: for whatsoever a man soweth, that shall he also reap."

Romans 12:14-21 says, "Bless them which persecute you: bless, and curse not. Rejoice with them that do rejoice, and weep with them that weep. Be of the same mind one toward another. Mind not high things, but condescend to men of low estate. Be not wise in your own conceits. Recompense to no man evil for evil. Provide things honest in the sight of all men. If it be possible, as much as lieth in you, live peaceably with all men. Dearly beloved, avenge not yourselves, but rather give place unto wrath: for it is written, Vengeance is mine; I will repay, saith the Lord. Therefore if thine enemy hunger, feed him; if he thirst, give him drink: for in so doing thou shalt heap coals of fire on his head. Be not overcome of evil, but overcome evil with good."

Remember, when we do good to others, good will come back to us.

Iron *Sharpens* Iron

Study Notes

Additional Scripture References:

Notes:

Iron *Sharpens* **Iron**

God Is More Than Enough

Dear Friend:

We serve the God who is "*more than enough*", and He wants us to have abundance in every area of our lives. Our God is the Creator of heaven and earth. He created the silver and gold and the cattle on the thousand hills (Psalm 50:10,12). God created all of this for His man Adam, and for all of the generations to come after Adam. But Adam sold out to Satan in the Garden of Eden, and he [Satan] became the god of this world [the world system].

Every since the time of Adam, Satan has been trying to keep God's people from succeeding and prospering. He tries to hold back the silver and gold from us, but the good news is that Jesus stripped Satan of all of his authority and he [Satan] no longer has any authority over us. We no longer have to worry about Satan trying to keep us from succeeding and prospering. We do not have to rely upon the world system to have our needs met and we don't have to worry about our needs going unmet. Every morning when we wake up, we shouldn't begin our day by worrying, instead we should start our day by saying:

> *Lord You are my Shepherd and I shall not want.*
> *You feed the birds of the air, and I know that You will feed me.*
> *I've never seen the righteous forsaken and their children begging for bread.*
> *Thank You Lord, You are more than enough for me.*

We must believe God and trust Him to meet all of our needs. He'll liberally supply for all of our needs. He has an abundant supply and He never runs out.

Psalm 23:1 says, "The Lord is my shepherd; I shall not want."

Philippians 4:19 says, "But my God shall supply all your need according to his riches in glory by Christ Jesus."

Psalm 37:25 says, "I have been young, and now am old; yet have I not seen the righteous forsaken, nor his seed begging bread."

Galatians 3:29 says, "And if ye be Christ's, then are ye Abraham's seed, and heirs according to the promise."

Psalm 103:2-5 says, "Bless the Lord, O my soul, and forget not all his benefits: Who forgiveth all thine iniquities; who healeth all thy diseases; Who redeemeth thy life from destruction; who crowneth thee with lovingkindness and tender mercies; Who satisfieth thy mouth with good things; so that thy youth is renewed like the eagle's."

Matthew 6:33 says, "But seek ye first the kingdom of God, and his righteousness; and all these things shall be added unto you."

Remember, God has all of the resources to meet all and any of our needs.

Iron *Sharpens* Iron

Study Notes

Additional Scripture References:

Notes:

Iron *Sharpens* Iron

The Holiday Season

Dear Friend:

The Holiday Season is the time of year when people feel more depressed and lonely than any other time of the year. Single women think that they'll never meet anyone. Single men hurriedly get engaged and marry within a matter of weeks, because they feel obligated.

No matter what our emotions or feelings tell us, we shouldn't be led by them. We must trust God to send the right person into our lives. We shouldn't marry just because we feel pressured or obligated. Too many people remedy their feelings of loneliness by making life long commitments. They may end up settling for second best and not God's best.

We must stop feeling depressed, lonely, and sorry for ourselves. We should think about how we can be a blessing to someone else. We can visit the nursing home and share Jesus with those whom we visit. We can bake cookies for a neighbor. We can cook for someone who's shut in. We can run errands, or do some other chores for the elderly in our community. As we begin to do good things for others, we'll find that we don't have time to feel lonely or depressed.

We should share the love of Jesus with everyone around us, and take the time to reflect on the birth of Jesus, and why He came to the earth. This is the true reason for the Holiday Season.

Isaiah 9:6 says, "For unto us a child is born, unto us a son is given: and the government shall be upon his shoulder: and his name shall be called Wonderful, Counsellor, The mighty God, The everlasting Father, The Prince of Peace."

John 3:16,17 says, "For God so loved the world, that he gave his only begotten Son, that whosoever believeth in him should not perish, but have everlasting life. For God sent not his Son into the world to condemn the world; but that the world through him might be saved."

Luke 4:18 says, "The Spirit of the Lord is upon me, because he hath anointed me to preach the gospel to the poor; he hath sent me to heal the brokenhearted, to preach deliverance to the captives, and recovering of sight to the blind, to set at liberty them that are bruised."

Remember, we should share the love of *Jesus* during the Holiday Season.

Iron *Sharpens* Iron

Study Notes

Additional Scripture References:

Notes:

Iron *Sharpens* Iron

God Is Faithful

Dear Friend:

Do you know we serve the God who is faithful? God is faithful to His Word and He is faithful to all of His promises. No matter what trial or tribulation we may be going through, God is faithful to deliver us.

When we are in the midst of trials and tribulations, the Word of God tells us that God is with us in trouble and He will deliver us (Psalm 91:15). If we are worried about how we are going to pay our bills, or not having enough money to make ends meet, the Word of God tells us that God will supply all of our needs (Philippians 4:19). If we need healing in our bodies and healing in our minds, the Word of God tells us that Jesus was wounded for our transgressions, and He was bruised for our iniquities, and the chastisement of our peace was upon Him, and by His stripes we are healed (Isaiah 53:3-5).

We must believe God, who is faithful, and all that He promised in His Word, He'll do. There's *NOTHING* too difficult for Him and there's *NOTHING* impossible for Him. We can count on the faithfulness of God.

Deuteronomy 7:9 says, "Know therefore that the Lord thy God, he is God, the faithful God, which keepeth covenant and mercy with them that love him and keep his commandments to a thousand generations."

1 Corinthians 10:13 says, "There hath no temptation taken you but such as is common to man: but God is faithful, who will not suffer you to be tempted above that ye are able; but will with the temptation also make a way to escape, that ye may be able to bear it."

2 Thessalonians 3:3 says, "But the Lord is faithful, who shall stablish you, and keep you from evil."

Hebrews 10:23 says, "Let us hold fast the profession of our faith without wavering; (for he is faithful that promised."

1 John 1:9 says, "If we confess our sins, he is faithful and just to forgive us our sins, and to cleanse us from all unrighteousness."

Numbers 23:19 says, "God is not a man, that he should lie; neither the son of man, that he should repent: hath he said, and shall he not do it? or hath he spoken, and shall he not make it good?"

Psalm 119:89,90 says, "For ever, O Lord, thy word is settled in heaven. Thy faithfulness is unto all generations: thou hast established the earth, and it abideth."

Remember, we can count on the *faithfulness* of God.

Iron *Sharpens* Iron

Study Notes

Additional Scripture References:

_____
_____
_____
_____
_____

Notes:

_____
_____
_____
_____
_____
_____
_____
_____
_____
_____
_____
_____
_____
_____
_____
_____
_____

Iron *Sharpens* Iron

The Integrity Of God's Word

Dear Friend:

The Bible tells us that we should know the truth, and the truth shall make us free (John 8:32). The Bible also tells us that the Word of God is truth (John 17:17). If the Word of God is truth, then the more we know the Word of God, the more it will make us free. The more we study and meditate upon the Word of God, the more freedom we will experience.

The Word of God is pure [tried and purified], and He is a shield to those that put their trust in Him (Proverbs 30:5). God's Word is not tainted, weak or polluted, and as we put our trust in Him, He will be a covering of protection for us.

The Word of God is quick and powerful, and it is sharper than any two-edged sword (Hebrews 4:12). God's Word is full of living power, and it is sharper than the sharpest dagger, cutting swift and deep, removing all of the junk out of our lives.

The Bible says, "As the rain and snow come down from heaven and stay upon the ground to water the earth, and cause the grain to grow and to produce seed for the farmer and bread for the hungry, so also is my Word. I send it out and it always produces fruit. It shall accomplish all I want it to, and prosper everywhere I send it." (Isaiah 55:10,11, The Living Bible). The Word of God is reliable and full of integrity. It is everlasting and it always brings results.

Psalm 12:6,7 says, "The words of the Lord are pure words: as silver tried in a furnace of earth, purified seven times. Thou shalt keep them, O Lord, thou shalt preserve them from this generation for ever."

Isaiah 55:11 says, "So shall my word be that goeth forth out of my mouth: it shall not return unto me void, but it shall accomplish that which I please, and it shall prosper in the thing whereto I sent it."

Hebrews 4:12 says, "For the word of God is quick, and powerful, and sharper than any twoedged sword, piercing even to the dividing asunder of soul and spirit, and of the joints and marrow, and is a discerner of the thoughts and intents of the heart."

Isaiah 55:10,11 says, "For as the rain cometh down, and the snow from heaven, and returneth not thither, but watereth the earth, and maketh it bring forth and bud, that it may give seed to the sower, and bread to the eater: So shall my word be that goeth forth out of my mouth: it shall not return unto me void, but it shall accomplish that which I please, and it shall prosper in the thing whereto I sent it."

Matthew 24:35 says, "Heaven and earth shall pass away, but my words shall not pass away."

Remember, we can always trust in the Word of God.

Iron *Sharpens* Iron

Study Notes

Additional Scripture References:

Notes:

Iron *Sharpens* Iron

Let Your Light Shine

Dear Friend:

I remembered a song I used to sing in Sunday school as a little girl. The lyrics are:

> *This little light of mine, I'm gonna let it shine.*
> *This little light of mine, I'm gonna let it shine.*
> *This little light of mine, I'm gonna let it shine.*
> *Let it shine. Let it shine. Let it shine.*
>
> *Everywhere I go, I'm gonna let it shine.*
> *Everywhere I go, I'm gonna let it shine.*
> *Everywhere I go, I'm gonna let it shine.*
> *Let it shine. Let it shine. Let it shine.*

As Christians, we should let our light shine throughout the world. Our light is Jesus living in us. The God of this world [Satan] has blinded the minds of the unbelievers, and they will continue to stay in darkness, if the light of the glorious Gospel of Christ isn't shone upon them.

We are the light of the world, and we should let our light shine before the world. We are the only light that the world will ever see, and this is why we should always exemplify Christ in our lives, so that the world may be won to Him. So we must let our light shine.

2 Corinthians 4:4-6 says, "In whom the god of this world hath blinded the minds of them which believe not, lest the light of the glorious gospel of Christ, who is the image of God, should shine unto them. For we preach not ourselves, but Christ Jesus the Lord; and ourselves your servants for Jesus' sake. For God, who commanded the light to shine out of darkness, hath shined in our hearts, to give the light of the knowledge of the glory of God in the face of Jesus Christ."

John 12:46 says, "I am come a light into the world, that whosoever believeth on me should not abide in darkness."

Matthew 5:14-16 says, "Ye are the light of the world. A city that is set on an hill can't be hid. Neither do men light a candle, and put it under a bushel, but on a candlestick; and it giveth light unto all that are in the house. Let your light so shine before men, that they may see your good works, and glorify your Father which is in heaven."

Philippians 1:27 says, "Only let your conversation be as it becometh the gospel of Christ: that whether I come and see you, or else be absent, I may hear of your affairs, that ye stand fast in one spirit, with one mind striving together for the faith of the gospel."

Remember, we must let our *light* shine.

Iron *Sharpens* Iron

Study Notes

Additional Scripture References:
_____
_____
_____
_____
_____
_____

Notes:
_____
_____
_____
_____
_____
_____
_____
_____
_____
_____
_____
_____
_____
_____
_____
_____
_____

Iron *Sharpens* Iron

The Heart Of God

Dear Friend:

The heart of God is people. God is interested in people, people being born into the Kingdom of God, people being reconciled to Him. The Word of God [the Bible] tells us that God so loved the world [people] that He gave His only begotten son [Jesus], and whoever believes in Him should have eternal life (John 3:16). God sacrificed Jesus upon the cross so that the world, through Christ, may be saved (John 3:17). It is through Christ's death that the world is reconciled to God.

As a child of God, we have the ministry of reconciliation. The ministry of reconciliation is God's call to the world [sinner] to come to Him just as they are to be reconciled unto Him. So as ministers of reconciliation, we must let the world know that Christ has died for their sins and has reconciled them back to God. God wants the world to know that they can come to Him, and He will not turn them away, because Jesus has paid the price for their sins when He died on Calvary.

John 12:40 in *The Amplified Bible* says, "He [Satan] has blinded their eyes and hardened and benumbed their [callous, degenerated] hearts [He has made their minds dull], to keep them from seeing with their eyes and understanding with their hearts and minds and repenting and turning to Me to heal them." The people in the world minds are blinded. They are lost and in darkness. We are the only vessels on earth that God can use to be a witness to the lost, bringing them over into the marvelous light of salvation. This touches the heart of God.

If we want to touch the heart of God, we should start today by letting the world know that they have been reconciled back to God. Their only task then is to confess Jesus as their Lord and Saviour.

John 12:46 says, "I am come a light into the world, that whosoever believeth on me should not abide in darkness."

2 Corinthians 5:18-21 says, "And all things are of God, who hath reconciled us to himself by Jesus Christ, and hath given to us the ministry of reconciliation; To wit, that God was in Christ, reconciling the world unto himself, not imputing their trespasses unto them; and hath committed unto us the word of reconciliation. Now then we are ambassadors for Christ, as though God did beseech you by us: we pray you in Christ's stead, be ye reconciled to God. For he hath made him to be sin for us, who knew no sin; that we might be made the righteousness of God in him."

Colossians 1:20,21 says, "And, having made peace through the blood of his cross, by him to reconcile all things unto himself; by him, I say, whether they be things in earth, or things in heaven. And you, that were sometime alienated and enemies in your mind by wicked works, yet now hath he reconciled."

Remember, we should have the heart of our Father God.

Iron *Sharpens* Iron

Study Notes

Additional Scripture References:

Notes:

Iron *Sharpens* Iron

It's Possible!

Dear Friend:

For several weeks, I've been thinking about the word, possible. I kept hearing those words inside of me: "It's possible, it's possible, it's possible for me. It's possible, it's possible and there's no impossibility". Do you know that as a child of God, all things are possible for us?

Yes, it's possible for us to change. It's possible for us to have all of our needs met. It's possible to have joy. It's possible to have peace. It's possible for that husband or wife to change. It's possible for that son or daughter to change. It's possible to have a good job. It's possible to have a nice home and a nice car.

The Word of God [the Bible] says, ". . . All things are possible to those that believe" (Mark 9:23). The Word also says, ". . . With God all things are possible" (Matthew 19:26). You know my friend, if God says that it's possible, than it's possible. We must believe what the Word of God says and obey it. When we call possible what God calls possible, it will become a reality.

Every time we look at a situation in our lives that may seem impossible to change, remember that the Word of God says, *"It's possible!"*

Let's make this confession out loud:

> *It's possible. It's possible. It's possible for me.*
> *It's possible. It's possible. God says it's possible.*
> *With God, there is no impossibility.*

Matthew 17:20 says, "And Jesus said unto them, Because of your unbelief: for verily I say unto you, If ye have faith as a grain of mustard seed, ye shall say unto this mountain, Remove hence to yonder place; and it shall remove; and nothing shall be impossible unto you."

Luke 1:37 says, "For with God nothing shall be impossible."

Mark 10:27 says, "And Jesus looking upon them saith, With men it is impossible, but not with God: for with God all things are possible."

Luke 18:27 says, "And he said, The things which are impossible with men are possible with God."

Remember, with God all things are *"possible"*.

Iron *Sharpens* Iron

Study Notes

Additional Scripture References:

Notes:

Iron *Sharpens* Iron

A New Millennium

Dear Friend:

As we enter into a new millennium, some of you might ask the question, "What does the new millennium holds for me?" It holds victories and blessings for us. It holds another level in God for us.

The new millennium holds victory over any battle, healing from any sickness or disease, provision for any lack, and answer to any prayer. *Hallelujah!* Let's take some time and think about that and give God some praise. We are going up another level in God.

In this new millennium, the Gospel will be spread in a greater measure, and God wants us to enter into the next level so that we can be part of spreading the Gospel in the whole world. If we are worried and concerned about sickness, disease, lack, and problems, we can't be effective in the spreading of the Gospel.

We should believe God and trust Him to bring us out of all of our troubles. The Lord will bring to past the things that we are believing and trusting Him for. So we don't have to worry or be concerned about anything. God is good, and He does all things good (Psalm 119:68).

I don't know about you, but I'm excited about the new millennium. God is shaking things up in the kingdom of darkness, and His people are being blessed beyond measure. The world will see the blessings upon us, and they will come to us, wanting to know more about our God. We should just live by God's Word, trust and believe Him, as He takes us to the next level into blessings and victories.

1 Corinthians 15:57 says, "But thanks be to God, which giveth us the victory through our Lord Jesus Christ."

Hebrews 13:5 says, "Let your conversation be without covetousness; and be content with such things as ye have: for he hath said, I will never leave thee, nor forsake thee."

Psalm 37:3-5 says, "Trust in the Lord, and do good; so shalt thou dwell in the land, and verily thou shalt be fed. Delight thyself also in the Lord; and he shall give thee the desires of thine heart. Commit thy way unto the Lord; trust also in him; and he shall bring it to pass."

Psalm 34:19 says, "Many are the afflictions of the righteous: but the Lord delivereth him out of them all."

Ephesians 3:20 says, "Now unto him that is able to do exceeding abundantly above all that we ask or think, according to the power that worketh in us."

Psalm 119:68 says, "Thou art good, and doest good; teach me thy statutes."

Remember, we are going up another level in God.

Iron *Sharpens* Iron

Study Notes

Additional Scripture References:

Notes:

Iron *Sharpens* Iron

Don't Try To Get Rich Too Fast

Dear Friend:

The Word of God [the Bible] speaks against getting rich too fast. There are some people who dwell on getting rich. They try all of the "*get rich quick*" schemes and gimmicks. Their motivation for getting rich is to get more things. They want the latest car, the biggest house, and all the clothes, jewelry, and shoes that they can get their hands on. They want to hoard up everything to themselves.

God will bless the work of our hands, and He'll cause us to get wealth through the work of our hands. Wealth obtained by honest work will last, but those who strive to get rich too fast will have wealth temporarily. One day they'll have it, and the next day it'll vanish like a puff of smoke that vanishes in thin air. The Word of God tells us to be content with our wages and be content with what we have (Hebrews 13:5).

Our real motivation for riches should be: to help build the Kingdom of God — we should keep the work of the Lord going for generations to come — to help those that are in need, and to be a blessing to our community. If we have the right motivation, riches will come to us.

Proverbs 13:7 says, "There is that maketh himself rich, yet hath nothing: there is that maketh himself poor, yet hath great riches."

Proverbs 13:11 says, "Wealth gotten by vanity shall be diminished: but he that gathereth by labour shall increase."

Luke 3:14 says, "And the soldiers likewise demanded of him, saying, And what shall we do? And he said unto them, Do violence to no man, neither accuse any falsely; and be content with your wages."

Proverbs 14:23 says, "In all labour there is profit: but the talk of the lips tendeth only to penury."

Hebrews 13:5 says, "Let your conversation be without covetousness; and be content with such things as ye have: for he hath said, I will never leave thee, nor forsake thee."

Proverbs 11:24,25 says, "There is that scattereth, and yet increaseth; and there is that withholdeth more than is meet, but it tendeth to poverty. The liberal soul shall be made fat: and he that watereth shall be watered also himself."

Proverbs 28:8 says, "He that by usury and unjust gain increaseth his substance, he shall gather it for him that will pity the poor."

Remember, do not *hasten* to get rich.

Iron *Sharpens* Iron

Study Notes

Additional Scripture References:

Notes:

Iron *Sharpens* Iron

The Best Is Yet To Come!

Dear Friend:

Many of us have gone through hard times in the past years. Some of us have encountered loss: loss of a loved one, loss of health, or loss of a job. Others have even thought about giving up on life, but this is not the time to be discouraged or give up. We are entering into a new year, a perfect time to make a fresh start.

We should decree that this year would be a year of prosperity, health and success for our loved ones and us. We should let this year be our best year ever! The things that weren't accomplished shouldn't be dropped or forgotten. We should bring them over into the new year with a plan to accomplish them.

We have to encourage and inspire ourselves to move forward with the dreams that God has given us. We must believe and trust God to bring them to past. David encouraged himself in the Lord (I Samuel 30:6). We should use David as our example, and encourage ourselves.

Let's make this decree out loud:

> *This year is a year to walk in the plan that God has for me.*
> *This year is a year of health, success, and prosperity for me.*
> *This year I will not be defeated, and I will not give up.*
> *God has great things in store for me this year.*

Hebrews 12:1,2 says, "Wherefore seeing we also are compassed about with so great a cloud of witnesses, let us lay aside every weight, and the sin which doth so easily beset us, and let us run with patience the race that is set before us, Looking unto Jesus the author and finisher of our faith; who for the joy that was set before him endured the cross, despising the shame, and is set down at the right hand of the throne of God."

Philippians 3:13,14 says, "Brethren, I count not myself to have apprehended: but this one thing I do, forgetting those things which are behind, and reaching forth unto those things which are before, I press toward the mark for the prize of the high calling of God in Christ Jesus."

Jeremiah 29:11-13 NIV says, "For I know the plans I have for you, declares the Lord, plans to prosper you and not to harm you, plans to give you hope and a future. Then you will call upon me and come and pray to me, and I will listen to you. You will seek me and find me when you seek me with all your heart."

Habakkuk 2:3 in *The Amplified Bible* says, "For the vision is yet for an appointed time and it hastens to the end [fulfillment]; it will not deceive or disappoint. Though it tarry, wait [earnestly] for it, because it will surely come; it will not be behindhand on its appointed day."

Remember, we should make this year our best year ever!

Iron *Sharpens* Iron

Study Notes

Additional Scripture References:

Notes:

Iron *Sharpens* Iron

God's Word Will Bring You Life

Dear Friend:

God's Word [the Bible] is life, and when we mix faith [confidence, trust, and action] with God's Word, it will bring us life. Psalm 16:11 says, "Thou wilt show me the path of life: in thy presence is fullness of joy; at thy right hand there are pleasures for evermore." Proverbs 4:22 says, "For they [the Word of God] are life unto those that find them, and health to all their flesh."

As born-again believers, we have eternal life, and that eternal life is working on the inside of us now. John 3:15,16 says, "That whosoever believeth in him should not perish, but have eternal life. For God so loved the world, that he gave his only begotten Son, that whosoever believeth in him should not perish, but have everlasting life."

Are you being challenged by sickness and disease? Begin to fill your mouth with God's Word and it will bring you life. God's Word will bring us life in any challenge that we may be facing. God's Word will quicken our bodies. "Quicken" means *to make alive, energy, vitality, full of life*.

Let's make this confession out loud:

> *God's Word brings me life. That life is working on the inside of me.*
> *It makes me alive and full of life. Rivers of life are flowing out of me.*
> *It drives out sickness and disease. I shall live and not die.*
> *I shall go forth and proclaim the works of the Lord.*

Romans 8:2 says, "For the law of the Spirit of life in Christ Jesus hath made me free from the law of sin and death."

Psalm 118:17 says, "I shall not die, but live, and declare the works of the Lord."

1 John 1:1 says, "That which was from the beginning, which we have heard, which we have seen with our eyes, which we have looked upon, and our hands have handled, of the Word of life."

Romans 8:11 says, "But if the Spirit of him that raised up Jesus from the dead dwell in you, he that raised up Christ from the dead shall also quicken your mortal bodies by his Spirit that dwelleth in you."

Psalm 16:11 says, "Thou wilt show me the path of life: in thy presence is fullness of joy; at thy right hand there are pleasures for evermore."

Psalm 36:9 says, "For with thee is the fountain of life: in thy light shall we see light."

Remember, God's Word is *full of life*.

Iron *Sharpens* Iron

Study Notes

Additional Scripture References:
_____
_____
_____
_____
_____

Notes:
_____
_____
_____
_____
_____
_____
_____
_____
_____
_____
_____
_____
_____
_____
_____
_____

Iron *Sharpens* Iron

The Outward Workings Of Love

Dear Friend:

The new commandment that Jesus left us is to love one another. John 13:34,35 says, "A new commandment I give unto you, That ye love one another; as I have loved you, that ye also love one another. By this shall all men know that ye are my disciples, if ye have love one to another."

Many of us have become self-centered. What I mean is, that we are centered only on what we can get, no matter whom we use or step on. Some of us got the "I've got mine, you get yours the best way you can" attitude. Is that the love of God?

Many of us love only those whom we choose to love. Have you ever heard this saying; "If you scratch my back, I'll scratch yours." Is that the love of God? God loves everybody. If we are going to be imitators of God, we should love everybody.

When we see someone who's hungry, do we feed them? When we see someone who's in need of clothes, do we clothe them? The bottom line is, that when we see someone who needs help, do we help them? How can we say we have the love of God, and not help others?

Love is an action, and we must put the love of God that's inside of us to action. As God demonstrated the outward workings of love toward us, we should demonstrate that same love toward others.

Matthew 25:42-45 says, "For I was an hungered, and ye gave me no meat: I was thirsty, and ye gave me no drink: I was a stranger, and ye took me not in: naked, and ye clothed me not: sick, and in prison, and ye visited me not. Then shall they also answer him, saying, Lord, when saw we thee an hungered, or athirst, or a stranger, or naked, or sick, or in prison, and did not minister unto thee? Then shall he answer them, saying, Verily I say unto you, Inasmuch as ye did it not to one of the least of these, ye did it not to me."

John 13:34,35 says, "A new commandment I give unto you, That ye love one another; as I have loved you, that ye also love one another. By this shall all men know that ye are my disciples, if ye have love one to another."

1 John 4:20,21 says, "If a man say, I love God, and hateth his brother, he is a liar: for he that loveth not his brother whom he hath seen, how can he love God whom he hath not seen? And this commandment have we from him, That he who loveth God love his brother also."

1 John 4:8,16 says, "He that loveth not knoweth not God; for God is love. And we have known and believed the love that God hath to us. God is love; and he that dwelleth in love dwelleth in God, and God in him."

Remember, we should love like God loves.

Iron *Sharpens* Iron

Study Notes

Additional Scripture References:

Notes:

Iron *Sharpens* Iron

Working The Word Of God

Dear Friend:

The Word of God [the Bible] works, but in order for the Word of God to work in our lives, we must work It. Some of you may be saying, "What do you mean by working the Word of God?" We must go to the Word of God and find Scriptures that cover our problems, confess and meditate upon those Scriptures, and believe that God will bring us the desired results. God's Word works, and it will bring us the desired results, if we do our part.

We shouldn't let the Word of God lay dormant in our hearts, but we should exercise it. We must exercise the Word of God in order to get results. For example, an athlete repetitiously goes through an exercise regimen to help him to develop strong muscles. He keeps applying the resistance of the weights against his muscles, until he is satisfied with the results. As Christians, we should learn from the athlete. We should take the spiritual regimen [which is the Word of God], and apply it against the resistance of the weights [test, trials and tribulations], until we are satisfied with the results [until we have the answer].

Some of us have been spiritual couch potatoes and spiritually lackadaisical. We must put an end to it today, and start applying the Word of God against our problems. God wants us to have the victory, and He wants us to get the desired results over all of our problems.

Psalm 119:105 says, "Thy word is a lamp unto my feet, and a light unto my path."

Psalm 119:154 says, "Plead my cause, and deliver me: quicken me according to thy word."

Luke 5:5,6 says, "And Simon answering said unto him, Master, we have toiled all the night, and have taken nothing: nevertheless at thy word I will let down the net. And when they had this done, they enclosed a great multitude of fishes: and their net brake."

John 2:5 says, "His mother saith unto the servants, Whatsoever he saith unto you, do it."

1 John 5:14,15 says, "And this is the confidence that we have in him, that, if we ask any thing according to his will, he heareth us: And if we know that he hear us, whatsoever we ask, we know that we have the petitions that we desired of him."

Psalm 34:19 says, "Many are the afflictions of the righteous: but the Lord delivereth him out of them all."

2 Corinthians 2:14 says, "Now thanks be unto God, which always causeth us to triumph in Christ, and maketh manifest the savour of his knowledge by us in every place."

James 1:22 says, "But be ye doers of the word, and not hearers only, deceiving your own selves."

Remember, God's Word works for us when we work God's Word.

Iron *Sharpens* Iron

Study Notes

Additional Scripture References:

Notes:

Iron *Sharpens* Iron

Jesus Is The Healer

Dear Friend:

Did you know that Jesus had a healing ministry on earth? Jesus went about doing good and healing all those who were oppressed of the devil (Acts 10:38). Jesus healed everyone who wanted to be healed (Luke 9:11, Matthew 8:16). The only ones that Jesus couldn't healed, where those who had unbelief (Mark 6:5,6).

Jesus is the Healer and His healing ministry is still at work in the earth today. There's not any reason for going around with sick, feeble bodies and unstable minds. Jesus wants us to be healed and He wants us to be whole. Jesus wants us healed and whole, so we can go everywhere proclaiming that He is the Healer and that He is still healing today.

Do you need healing in your body? Do you need healing in your mind? Let's go to the Lord in prayer and ask Him for healing:

> *Dear Jesus, I ask You to heal my body and make my mind sound.*
> *I believe that You are the Healer, and I believe in Your healing ministry.*
> *Thank You Jesus, I receive Your healing power in my body and mind.*
> *Your healing power is now at work in my body and in my mind.*

Isaiah 53:5 says, "But he was wounded for our transgressions, he was bruised for our iniquities: the chastisement of our peace was upon him; and with his stripes we are healed."

1 Peter 2:24 says, "Who his own self bare our sins in his own body on the tree, that we, being dead to sins, should live unto righteousness: by whose stripes ye were healed."

Matthew 8:16,17 says, "When the even was come, they brought unto him many that were possessed with devils: and he cast out the spirits with his word, and healed all that were sick: That it might be fulfilled which was spoken by Esaias the prophet, saying, Himself took our infirmities, and bare our sicknesses."

Psalm 107:19,20 says, "Then they cry unto the Lord in their trouble, and he saveth them out of their distresses. He sent his word, and healed them, and delivered them from their destructions."

Luke 6:17-19 says, "And he came down with them, and stood in the plain, and the company of his disciples, and a great multitude of people out of all Judaea and Jerusalem, and from the sea coast of Tyre and Sidon, which came to hear him, and to be healed of their diseases; And they that were vexed with unclean spirits: and they were healed. And the whole multitude sought to touch him: for there went virtue out of him, and healed them all."

Remember, Jesus is still healing today.

Iron *Sharpens* Iron

Study Notes

Additional Scripture References:

Notes:

Iron *Sharpens* Iron

Walking In Favor

Dear Friend:

As I was reading my Bible, I ran across the word, "favor". What is favor? The Webster Collegiate Dictionary defines "favor" as *to do a kindness for, endow*. Favor is simply *the grace of God*.

Have you ever gone to a store to purchase a particular item or items, and those items were marked down 50%? As you go to the counter to purchase those items, the salesperson says, "These items will be marked down an additional 25% later this evening, but I will let you take advantage of the marked down price now". This happens to me so many times.

Have you ever had someone to provide a particular service for you, and the person who's providing the service says, "I don't know why I'm letting you have this service for this price". But I know why. It is the favor of God. Have you ever received an unexpected raise or promotion on your job? Have you ever had blessings heaped upon you? That's the favor of God! God's favor allows us to receive acts of kindness and blessings from others.

Has the favor of God been operating in your life? If not, start saying, "I have favor with God and man". As you continue to say and believe that you have favor, one day you will begin to notice the favor of God at work in your life.

Proverbs 3:1-4 says, "My son, forget not my law; but let thine heart keep my commandments: For length of days, and long life, and peace, shall they add to thee. Let not mercy and truth forsake thee: bind them about thy neck; write them upon the table of thine heart: So shalt thou find favour and good understanding in the sight of God and man."

Genesis 39:2,3 says, "And the Lord was with Joseph, and he was a prosperous man; and he was in the house of his master the Egyptian. And his master saw that the Lord was with him, and that the Lord made all that he did to prosper in his hand."

Esther 2:15-17 says, "Now when the turn of Esther, the daughter of Abihail the uncle of Mordecai, who had taken her for his daughter, was come to go in unto the king, she required nothing but what Hegai the king's chamberlain, the keeper of the women, appointed. And Esther obtained favour in the sight of all them that looked upon her. So Esther was taken unto king Ahasuerus into his house royal in the tenth month, which is the month Tebeth, in the seventh year of his reign. And the king loved Esther above all the women, and she obtained grace and favour in his sight more than all the virgins; so that he set the royal crown upon her head, and made her queen instead of Vashti."

Psalm 5:12 says, "For thou, Lord, wilt bless the righteous; with favour wilt thou compass him as with a shield."

Remember to expect to receive acts of kindness and special benefits from others.

Conclusion

I pray that this book has encouraged and inspired you. This book should not only be used one time, but over and over again. As you continue to read this book, you will see things from the Scriptures that you haven't seen before, and your life will begin to be transformed and sharpened. You'll become a person that's full of faith and power!

If this book has been a blessing to you, consider sharing it with others so they too, can be encouraged, inspired and sharpened.

"Iron sharpeneth iron; so a man sharpeneth the countenance of his friend."

Proverbs 27:17

About The Author

Gerri Nash loves to encourage people and tell them that they can reach their full potential in God, and do everything that God has created them to do. Gerri also tells them that God has a plan for each one of us to fulfill and a purpose for our lives.

Gerri holds a Bachelor of Science degree in Computer Science with a minor in Mathematics from Southern University in Baton Rouge, Louisiana. She is also a graduate of RHEMA Bible Training Center in Broken Arrow, Oklahoma where she was trained in the Pastorate ministry.

Gerri works along side her husband, Corbin, who is the pastor of *COME* Church and founder of The Christian Outreach Ministries Evangelist (*COME*) in Tulsa, Oklahoma.

Product Information

The following are additional books published by COME Ministries:

<u>Books by Rev. Corbin Nash</u>
Take Your Victory
Who Are You
The Trying of Your Faith

To obtain additional copies of books and tapes, or schedule for a ministry engagement, please contact us at our website at www.comeministries.org, or write:

COME Ministries
P.O. Box 581942
Tulsa, Oklahoma 74158-1942
918.496.9555